Sopho

Ajax,
The Women of
Trachis,
Electra & Philoctetes

by

Sophocles

www.books.com.co

First Printing March 2016
Printed in the United States of America.
10 9 8 7 6 5 4 3 2 1

If this is a work of fiction, it is not meant to depict, portray or represent any particular real persons. All the characters, incidents and dialogues are the products of the author's imagination and are not to be construed as real. Any references or similarities to actual events, entities, real people, living or dead, or to real locales are intended to give the novel a sense of reality. Any similarity in other names, characters, entities, places and incidents is entirely coincidental.

LG Classics
New York, New York
www.books.com.co

TABLE OF CONTENTS

AJAX

Dramatis Personae

ATHENA
ODYSSEUS
AJAX
CHORUS OF SALAMINIANS
TECMESSA, concubine of AJAX
MESSENGER
TEUCER, half-brother of AJAX
MENELAUS
AGAMEMNON Mute Persons
EURYSACES, child of AJAX and TECMESSA
Attendants, Heralds, etc.

Before the tent of AJAX in the Greek camp at Troy. It is dawn. ODYSSEUS is discovered examining the ground before the tent. ATHENA appears from above.

ATHENA Son of Laertes, ever do I behold thee Scheming to snatch some vantage o'er thy foes. And now among the tents that guard the ships Of Ajax, camped at the army's outmost verge, Long have I watched thee hunting in his trail, And scanning his fresh prints, to learn if now He be within or forth. Skilled in the chase Thou seemest, as a keen-nosed Spartan hound. For the man but now has passed within, his face And slaughterous hands streaming with sweat and blood. No further need for thee to peer about Inside these doors. But say what eager quest Is thine, that I who know may give thee light.

ODYSSEUS Voice of Athena, dearest of Gods to me, How clearly, though thou be invisible, Do I hear thy call, and seize it with my soul, As when a bronze-mouthed Tyrrhene trumpet sounds! Rightly thou judgest that on a foe's trail, Broad-shielded Ajax, I range to and fro. Him, and no other, I have long been tracking. This very night against us he has wrought A deed incredible, if in truth 'tis he. For we know nothing sure, but drift in doubt. Gladly I assumed the burden of this task. For not long since we found that our whole spoil Had been destroyed, both herds and flocks, slaughtered By some man's hand, their guardians dead beside them. Now 'tis on him that all men lay this guilt: And a scout who had seen him swiftly bounding Across the plain alone with reeking sword, Informed me and bore witness. I forthwith, Darting in hot chase, now pick out his tracks, But now, bewildered, know not whose they are. Timely thou comest. As in past days, so In days to come I am guided by thy hand.

ATHENA I know it, Odysseus: so on the path betimes A sentinel friendly to thy chase I came.

ODYSSEUS Dear mistress, do I labour to good purpose?

ATHENA Know 'twas by yonder man these deeds were wrought.

ODYSSEUS And why did he so brandish a frenzied hand?

ATHENA In grievous wrath for Achilles' panoply.

ODYSSEUS Why then upon the flocks did he make this onslaught?

ATHENA Your blood he deemed it was that stained his hand.

ODYSSEUS Was this outrage designed against the Greeks?

ATHENA He had achieved it too, but for my vigilance.

ODYSSEUS What bold scheme could inspire such reckless daring?

ATHENA By night he meant to steal on you alone.

ODYSSEUS Did he come near us? Did he reach his goal?

ATHENA He stood already at the two chiefs' doors.

ODYSSEUS What then withheld his eager hand from bloodshed?

ATHENA 'Twas I restrained him, casting on his eyes O'ermastering notions of that baneful ecstasy, That turned his rage on flocks and mingled droves Of booty yet unshared, guarded by herdsmen. Then plunging amid the thronging horns he slew, Smiting on all sides; and one while he fancied The Atreidae were the captives he was slaughtering, Now 'twas some other chief on whom he fell. And I, while thus he raved in maniac throes, Urged him on, drove him into the baleful toils. Thereafter, when he had wearied of such labours, He bound with thongs such oxen as yet lived, With all the sheep, and drove them to his tents, As though his spoil were men, not horned cattle. Now lashed together in the hut he tortures them. But to thee too will I expose this madness, That seeing thou mayst proclaim it to all the Greeks. Boldly await him here, nor apprehend Mischance; for I will turn aside his eyes, Foiling his vision lest he see thy face. (She calls to AJAX within the tent.) Hearken, thou who art pinioning with cords The wrists of captives; hither, I bid thee, come. Thou, Ajax, hear me: come to thy tent's door.

ODYSSEUS What dost thou, Athena? Do not summon him forth.

ATHENA Abide in silence. Earn not the name of coward.

ODYSSEUS Nay, by the Gods, let him remain within.

ATHENA What dost thou dread? Was he not once a

man?

ODYSSEUS Yes, and to me a foeman, and still is.

ATHENA To mock foes, is not that the sweetest mockery?

ODYSSEUS I am content he should remain indoors.

ATHENA To look upon a madman art thou afeard?

ODYSSEUS Had he been sane, no fear had made me shrink.

ATHENA Even now he shall not see thee, near as thou art.

ODYSSEUS How so, if still with the same eyes he sees?

ATHENA His orbs will I make dark, though vision is theirs.

ODYSSEUS Well, all is possible, when 'tis a god contrives.

ATHENA Stand then silent, abiding as thou art.

ODYSSEUS Stay I must; yet I fain would be far hence.

ATHENA Ho, Ajax! Once again I summon thee. So slight is thy regard for thine ally? (AJAX appears in the tent door, with a blood-stained scourge in his hand.)

AJAX Oh hail, Athena! Hail thou Zeus-born maid! Nobly hast thou stood by me. Now will I crown thee With trophies all of gold for this rich conquest.

ATHENA Thy words are welcome. But now tell me this: Hast thou dyed well thy sword in the Argive host?

AJAX Such vaunt is mine. I disclaim not that glory.

ATHENA Against the Atreidae didst thou arm thy hand?

AJAX So that Ajax nevermore shall they insult.

ATHENA The men are dead, if rightly I take thy meaning.

AJAX Yes, dead. Now let them rob me of my arms.

ATHENA 'Tis well. And what then of Laertes' son? In what plight does he stand? Or has he escaped thee?

AJAX Wouldst thou know where is that accursed fox?

ATHENA Even so-Odysseus, thine old adversary.

AJAX Goddess, a most dear captive in my tent He sits. I do not mean him to die yet.

ATHENA Till thou hast done what, gained what further vantage?

AJAX Till bound fast to a pillar beneath my roof-

ATHENA What evil wilt thou inflict on the poor wretch?

AJAX His back the scourge must crimson ere he dies.

ATHENA Nay, do not torture so the wretched man.

AJAX Athena, in all else will I do thy will; But his shall be no other doom than this.

ATHENA Thou then, since thy delight is to act thus, Smite, spare not, abate nought of thy intent.

AJAX To my work I return: and thus I charge thee, As now, so always fight thou upon my side. (AJAX goes back into the tent.)

ATHENA Seest thou, Odysseus, how great the strength of gods?

Whom couldst thou find more prudent than this man, Or whom in act more valiant, when need called?

ODYSSEUS I know none nobler; and I pity him In his misery, albeit he is my foe, Since he is yoked fast to an evil doom. My own lot I regard no less than his. For I see well, nought else are we but mere Phantoms, all we that live, mere fleeting shadows.

ATHENA Warned therefore by his fate, never do thou Thyself utter proud words against the gods; Nor swell with insolence, if thou shouldst vanquish Some rival by main strength or by wealth's power. For a day can bring all mortal greatness low, And a day can lift it up. But the gods love The wise of heart, the froward they abhor. (ATHENA vanishes and ODYSSEUS departs. The CHORUS OF SALAMINIANS enters.)

CHORUS (singing) Son of Telamon, lord of Salamis' isle,

On its wave-washed throne mid the breaking sea, I rejoice when fair are thy fortunes: But whene'er thou art smitten by the stroke of Zeus, Or the vehement blame of the fierce-tongued Greeks, Then sore am I grieved, and for fear I quake, As a fluttering dove with a scared eye. Even so by rumour murmuring loud Of the night late-spent our ears are assailed. 'Tis a tale of shame, how thou on the plains Where the steeds roam wild, didst ruin the Danaan Flocks and herds, Our spear-won booty as yet unshared, With bright sword smiting and slaughtering. Such now are the slanders Odysseus forges And whispers abroad into all men's ears, Winning easy belief: so specious the tale He is spreading against thee; and each new hearer Rejoices more than he who told, Exulting in thy degradation. For the shaft that is aimed at the noble of soul Smites home without fail: but whoe'er should accuse me Of such misdeeds, no faith would he win. 'Tis the stronger whom creeping jealousy strikes. Yet small men reft of help from the mighty Can ill be trusted to guard their walls. Best prosper the lowly in league with the great; And the great have need to be served by the less. But none to the knowledge of such plain truths May lead minds witless and froward. Even such are the men who murmur against thee: And vainly without thine aid, O King, We strive to repel their accusing hate. For whene'er they are safe from the scorn of thy glance,

They chatter and screech like bids in a flock: But smitten with dread of the powerful vulture, Doubtless at once, should'st thou but appear, They will cower down dumbly in silence.

(strophe)

Was it the Tauric Olympian Artemis, (Oh, the dread rumour of woe, Parent of my grievous shame!) Who drove thee forth to slaughter the herds of the people,

In wrath perchance for some unpaid-for victory, Whether defrauded of glorious spoil, or offerings Due for a stag that was slain? Or did the bronze-clad Demon of battle, aggrieved On him who scorned the might of his succouring spear, Plot revenge by nightly deception?

(antistrophe)

Ne'er of itself had thy heart, son of Telamon, Strayed into folly so far As to murder flocks and herds. Escape from heaven-sent madness is none: yet Apollo And Zeus avert these evil rumours of the Greeks. But should the story be false, these crafty slanders Spread by the powerful kings, And by the child of the infamous Sisyphid line, No more, my master, thus in the tent by the sea Hide thy countenance, earning an ill fame.

(epode)

Nay, but arise from thy seat, where'er so long wrapt in

Brooding pause from the battle thou hast lurked: arise, Heaven-high kindle the flame of death. But the insolence of thy foes boldly Thus wanders abroad in the wind-swept glens. Meanwhile all men mocking With venomous tongues taunt thee: But grief in my heart wanes not. (TECMESSA enters. The following lines between TECMESSA and the CHORUS are chanted responsively.)

TECMESSA Liegemen of Ajax, ship-companions, Ye children of earth-sprung Erechthid race, Lamentation is now our portion, to whom Dear is the far-off house of Telamon, Now that the stern and terrible Ajax Lies whelmed by a storm Of turbid wildering fury.

CHORUS To what evil change from the day's woe now Has night given birth? Thou daughter of Phrygian Teleutas, speak; For a constant love has valiant Ajax Borne thee, his spear-won prisoner bride. Then hide from us nought that thou knowest.

TECMESSA How to utter a tale of unspeakable things! For disastrous as death is the hap you will hear. In the darkness of night madness has seized Our glorious Ajax: he is ruined and lost. Hereof in the tent may proof be seen; Sword-slain victims in their own blood bathed, By his hand sacrificially slaughtered.

CHORUS (strophe)

What tidings of the fiery warrior tellest thou, Not to be borne, nor yet to be disputed, Rumoured abroad by the chiefs of the Danaan host, Mightily still spreading and wax-ing! Woe's me! I dread the horror to come. Yea, to a public death doomed

Will he die, if in truth his be the hand that wielded The red sword that in frenzy hath slain the herds and mounted herdsmen.

TECMESSA Ah me! Thence was it, thence that he came to me

Leading his captive flock from the pastures! Thereof in the tent some did he slaughter, Others hewed he asunder with slashing sword; Then he caught up amain two white-footed rams, Sliced off from the one both the head and the tongue, And flings them away; But the other upright to a pillar he binds, Then seizing a heavy horse-harnessing thong He smites with the whistling doubled lash, Uttering fierce taunts which an evil fiend No mere mortal could have taught him.

CHORUS (antistrophe)

'Tis time that now each with shamefully muffled head

Forth from the camp should creep with stealthy footsteps.

Nay, on the ship let us muster, and benched at the oars
Over the waves launch her in swift flight. Such angry threats
sound in our ears hurled by the brother princes,

The Atreidae: and I quake, fearing a death by stoning,
The dread portion of all who would share our hapless master's ruin.

TECMESSA Yet hope we: for ceased is the lightning's
flash:

His rage dies down like a fierce south-wind. But now,
grown sane, new misery is his; For on woes self-wrought he
gazes aghast, Wherein no hand but his own had share; And
with anguish his soul is afflicted.

LEADER OF THE CHORUS Nay, if 'tis ceased, there is
good cause to hope. Once 'tis past, of less moment is his
frenzy.

TECMESSA And which, were the choice thine, wouldst
thou prefer,

To afflict thy friends and feel delight thyself, Or to share
sorrow, grieving with their grief?

LEADER The twofold woe, lady, would be the greater.

TECMESSA Then we, though plagued no more, are undone now.

LEADER What mean thy words? Their sense is dark to
me.

TECMESSA Yonder man, while his spirit was diseased,
Himself had joy in his own evil plight, Though to us, who
were sane, he brought distress. But now, since he has respite from his plague, He with sore grief is utterly cast down,
And we likewise, no less than heretofore. Are there not here
two woes instead of one?

LEADER Yes truly. And I fear, from some god came This

stroke; how else? if, now his frenzy is ceased, His mind has no more ease than when it raged.

TECMESSA 'Tis even as I said, rest well assured.

LEADER But how did this bane first alight upon him? To us who share thy grief show what befell.

TECMESSA Thou shalt hear all, as though thou hadst been present.

In the middle of the night, when the evening braziers No longer flared, he took a two-edged sword, And fain would sally upon an empty quest. But I rebuked him, saying: "What doest thou, Ajax? Why thus uncalled wouldst thou go forth? No messenger has summoned thee, no trumpet Roused thee. Nay, the whole camp is sleeping still." But curtly he replied in well-worn phrase: "Woman, silence is the grace of woman." Thus schooled, I yielded; and he rushed out alone. What passed outside the tent, I cannot tell. But in he came, driving lashed together Bulls, and shepherd dogs, and fleecy prey. Some he beheaded, the wrenched-back throats of some He slit, or cleft their chines; others he bound And tortured, as though men they were, not beasts. Last, darting through the doors, as to some phantom He tossed words, now against the Atreidae, now Taunting Odysseus, piling up huge jeers Of how he had gone and wreaked his scorn upon them. Soon he rushed back within the tent, where slowly And hardly to his reason he returned. And gazing round on the room filled with havoc, He struck his head and cried out; then amidst The wrecks of slaughtered sheep a wreck he fell, And sat clutching his hair with tight-clenched nails. There first for a long while he crouched speechless; Then did he threaten me with fearful threats, If I revealed not all that had befallen him, Asking what meant the plight wherein he lay. And I, friends, terror-stricken, told him all That had been done, so far as I had knowledge. Forthwith he broke forth into bitter wailing, Such as I ne'er had heard from him before For always had he held that such laments Befitted cowards only, and low-souled men: But uttering no shrill cries, he would express His grief in low groans, as of a moaning bull.

But now prostrate beneath so great a woe, Not tasting food nor drink, he sits among The sword-slain beasts, motionless where he sank. And plainly he meditates some baleful deed, For so portend his words and lamentations. But, O friends!- 'twas for this cause I came forth- Enter and help, if help at all you can: For by friends' words men so bestead are won.

LEADER Child of Teleutas, fearful are thy tidings, That our prince has been maddened by his griefs.

AJAX (within) Alas! Woe, woe!

TECMESSA Soon, I fear, worse will follow. Heard you not?

'Twas Ajax. Oh, how dreadful was that cry.

AJAX Alas! Woe, woe!

LEADER He seems either still frenzied, or else grieving

For his past frenzies, now he sees their work.

AJAX Alas! My son, my son!

TECMESSA Woe's me! Eurysaces, 'tis for thee he calls. What can he purpose?-Where art thou?-Ah, woe!

AJAX Teucer, come!-Where is Teucer? Will he never Come back from cattle-raiding?-while I perish!

LEADER He seems in his right mind. But open the doors. Perhaps even the sight of me may sober him. (She opens the doors of the tent. AJAX is revealed sitting among the slain beasts.)

TECMESSA See, I have opened. You may now behold What he has done, and in what plight he lies.

AJAX (chanting) Alas! My shipmates and friends, you that alone to me Loyal and true remain, of all friends alone, Behold how great a billow lately rising from the storm of blood

Surging around engulphs me!

LEADER Ah me, too true, it seems, was thy report. This sight reveals the work of no sane mind.

AJAX (chanting) Alas! My mates, skilled and tried in brave seamanship, Ye who embarking drove the wave-cleaving oar, In you, in you alone I see a help and refuge from despair.

Smite me, and spill my blood too.

LEADER Keep silence from dread words; nor curing ill By ill, so swell the misery of this curse.

AJAX (chanting) Behold now the bold, the man stout of heart,

Who ne'er shrank in fight against foes-behold How I have spent my rage on beasts that feared no harm! Ah me, the mockery! To what shame am I brought low

TECMESSA Ajax, my master, I entreat thee, speak not so.

AJAX (chanting) Away hence, I command thee! Take thyself elsewhere.

Aiai! Aiai!

LEADER Oh, by the Gods, we pray thee, yield to wisdom's voice.

AJAX (chanting) Oh, wretch that I was to allow Those cursed foes to slip from my hands, and assaulting Horned kine and goodly flocks, madly to spill Their life in streams of dark blood!

LEADER Why still be afflicted, now the deed is done past cure?

Never can these things be as though they had not been.

AJAX (chanting) Thou all-spying knave, of all deeds of shame

The prompt, easy tool, Odysseus the wise! Villain, of all

the camp the most foul and vile! Huge laughter doubtless shakes thee now for sheer delight.

LEADER As God appoints, so every man laughs or laments.

AJAX (chanting) Would I might meet him, crushed and broken though I be. Alas! Woe, woe!

LEADER Speak no proud words. Seest thou not to what woe thou art sunk?

AJAX (chanting) O Zeus, of my fathers the sire, Might I but kill that hateful and crafty dissembler, Yea, and those two brother kings, partners in pride, Then last myself too perish!

TECMESSA If thus thou prayest, pray therewith for me, that

Die with thee. Why, when thou art dead, should I live on?

AJAX (chanting) Alas! Shadow that art my light! Erebus, oh to me verily bright as day! Receive, receive me your habitant. Receive me now no more worthy to seek help of the gods, Nor any more from fellow mortal men to claim kindness: No, but she the strong Zeus-born deity Miserably tortures me. Whither should I then flee? Whither seek for rest? Since my former glory is gone, my friends, With yonder victims, yonder spoils by frenzy won, Since all the host with swords uplifted Sternly would slay me,

TECMESSA Ah, woe is me! from such a noble warrior To hear such words as once he ne'er had deigned to speak!

AJAX (chanting) Alas! Billowy paths of foam, Eddying caves, and ye coppices by the shore, A weary, weary time tarrying here Beneath the walls of Troy me have you kept, but from this hour

Alive you shall not keep me. Truth I speak: let none doubt it.

O Scamander's wave, Stream whose neighbouring flow
Oft have the Argives blest, Never, nevermore Me shall you
behold, Me (a proud word will I utter now) Whose peer in
battle Troy has never seen yet come From Hellas' land: but
now dishonoured Thus am I prostrate.

LEADER In truth I know not how to restrain thy speech,
nor yet

To suffer it; so grievous is thy couch of woe.

AJAX Aiai! Who ever would have thought my name
Would harmonise so aptly with my woes? For now well may
I wail that sound out twice, Yea thrice; such woeful destinies
are mine, Whose father from this land of Ida won Fame's
noblest guerdon over the whole host, And crowned with
praises only sailed back home; But I, his son, who to the
self-same Troy Came after him, in might no less than he,
Nor rendering meaner service by my deeds, Dishonoured by
the Argives perish thus. Yet this methinks I know for truth,
were now Achilles living and called on to adjudge As the
award of valour his own arms, No man's hand would have
grasped them before mine. But now the Atreidae to a scheming knave Have dealt them, thrusting by my valiant deeds.
And if these eyes, these wits had not in frenzy Swerved
from my purpose, never would they thus Pervert judgment
against another man. But the irresistible fierce-eyed goddess, even As I was arming my right hand to slay them,
Foiled me, smiting me with a maddening plague, So that I
stained my hand butchering these cattle. Thus my foes mock
me, escaped beyond my reach, Through no goodwill of mine:
but if a god Thwart vengeance, even the base may escape the
nobler. And what should I now do, who manifestly To Heav-
en am hateful; whom the Greeks abhor, Whom every Trojan
hates, and this whole land? Shall I desert the beached ships,
and abandoning The Atreidae, sail home o'er the Aegean
sea? With what face shall I appear before my father Telamon? How will he find heart to look On me, stripped of my
championship in war, That mighty crown of fame that once
was his? No, that I dare not. Shall I then assault Troy's
fortress, and alone against them all Achieve some glorious

exploit and then die? No, I might gratify the Atreidae thus. That must not be. Some scheme let me devise Which may prove to my aged sire that I, His son, at least by nature am no coward. For 'tis base for a man to crave long life Who endures never-varying misery. What joy can be in day that follows day, Bringing us close then snatching us from death? As of no worth would I esteem that man Who warms himself with unsubstantial hopes. Nobly to live, or else nobly to die Befits proud birth. There is no more to say.

LEADER The word thou hast uttered, Ajax, none shall call

Bastard, but the true offspring of thy soul. Yet pause. Let those who love thee overrule Thy resolution. Put such thoughts aside.

TECMESSA O my lord Ajax, of all human ills Greatest is fortune's wayward tyranny. Of a free father was I born the child, One rich and great as any Phrygian else. Now am I a slave; for so the gods, or rather Thy warrior's hand, would have it. Therefore since I am thy bedfellow, I wish thee well, And I entreat thee by domestic Zeus, And by the embraces that have made me thine, Doom me not to the cruel taunts of those Who hate thee, left a bond-slave in strange hands. For shouldst thou perish and forsake me in death, That very day assuredly I to Shall be seized by the Argives, with thy son To endure henceforth the portion of a slave. Then one of my new masters with barbed words Shall wound me scoffing: "See the concubine Of Ajax, who was mightiest of the host, What servile tasks are hers who lived so daintily!" Thus will men speak, embittering my hard lot, But words of shame for thee and for thy race. Nay, piety forbid thee to forsake Thy father in his drear old age-thy mother With her sad weight of years, who many a time Prays to the gods that thou come home alive. And pity, O king, thy son, who without thee To foster his youth, must live the orphaned ward Of loveless guardians. Think how great a sorrow Dying thou wilt bequeath to him and me. For I have nothing left to look to more Save thee. By thy spear was my country ravaged; And by another stroke did fate lay low My mother and my sire to dwell with Hades. Without thee then what fatherland were mine? What wealth? On thee alone rests all my hope. O take thought for me too. Do we not owe Remembrance, where we have met with any joy? For kindness begets kindness ever-more But he who from whose mind fades the memory Of benefits, noble is he no more.

LEADER Ajax, would that thy soul would feel compassion,

As mine does; so wouldst thou approve her words.

AJAX Verily my approval shall she win, If only she find heart to do my bidding.

TECMESSA Dear Ajax, in all things will I obey.

AJAX Then bring me here my son, for I would see him.

TECMESSA Nay, but I sent him from me in my fears.

AJAX During my late affliction, is that thy meaning?

TECMESSA Lest by ill chance he should meet thee and so perish.

AJAX Yes, that would have been worthy of my fate.

TECMESSA That at least I was watchful to avert.

AJAX I praise thine act and the foresight thou hast shown.

TECMESSA Since that is so, what shall I do to serve thee?

AJAX Let me speak to him and behold his face.

TECMESSA He is close by in the attendants' charge.

AJAX Why is his coming then so long delayed?

TECMESSA (calling) My son, thy father calls thee.-Bring him thither

Whichever of you is guiding the child's steps.

AJAX Is the man coming? Has he heard thy call?

TECMESSA See, he is here already with the child. (An attendant enters, leading the child, EURYSACES.)

AJAX Lift him up, lift him hither. He will not shrink In terror at sight of yonder new-spilt blood, If he be rightly mine, his father's son. Early must he be broken to his sire's Stern rugged code, and grow like-natured with him. O son, mayst thou prove happier than thy father, In all else like him, and thou'lt prove not base. Yet even now might I envy thee herein, That of these woes thou hast no sense at all. For the life that is unconscious is most sweet- Until we learn what joy and sorrow are. But that once learnt, then midst thy father's foes Thou must show what thou art, and of what breed. Till then be nurtured on soft airs, cherishing Thy tender life, and be thy mother's joy. None of the Greeks, I know, will do thee wrong With cruel outrage, even though I be gone. So trusty a guardian will I leave thee, Teucer, Who will not stint his loving care, though now He is gone far away, in chase of foes. But you, my warriors, comrades in seafaring, On you too I impose this task of love; And fail not to announce my will to Teucer, That to my home he take the child and show him To Telamon and my mother Eriboea, That henceforth he may comfort their old age. And charge him that no game-steward make my arms A prize for the Greeks-nor he who ruined me. But this take thou, my son Eurysaces; Hold it and wield it by its firm-stitched thong, This sevenfold spear-proof shield, whence comes thy name.

But else with me my arms shall be interred. (Speaking now to TECMESSA) Come, take the child hence quickly, and bolt the doors:

And let there be no weeping and lamenting Before the hut. Women love tears too well. Close quickly. It is not for a skilful leech To drone charms o'er a wound that craves the knife.

LEADER I am fearful, listening to this eager mood. The sharp edge of thy tongue, I like it not.

TECMESSA O my lord Ajax, what art thou purposing?

AJAX Question me not. To be discreet is best.

TECMESSA Ah me, heavy is my heart. Now by thy child,
By the gods, I entreat, forsake us not.

AJAX Vex me no further. Know'st thou not that I To the
gods owe no duty any more?

TECMESSA Utter no proud words.

AJAX Speak to those who listen.

TECMESSA Wilt thou not heed?

AJAX Too much thou hast spoken already.

TECMESSA Yes, through my fears, O king.

AJAX Close the doors quickly.

TECMESSA For the gods' love, relent.

AJAX 'Tis a foolish hope, If thou shouldst now propose
to school my mood. (The doors are closed upon AJAX. TEC-
MESSA goes out with EURYSACES.)

CHORUS (singing, strophe 1)

O famed Salamis, thou amidst Breaking surges abidest
ever Blissful, a joy to the eyes of all men. But I the while
long and wearily tarrying Through countless months still
encamped on the fields of Ida

In misery here have made my couch, By time broken and
worn, In dread waiting the hour When I shall enter at last
the terrible shadow abode of Hades.

(antistrophe 1)

Now dismays me a new despair, This incurable frenzy
(woe, ah Woe's me!) cast by the gods on Ajax, Whom thou of
old sentest forth from thy shores, a strong

And valiant chief; but now, to his friends a sore grief,

Devouring his lonely heart he sits. His once glorious deeds Are now fallen and scorned, Fallen to death without love from the loveless and pitiless sons of Atreus.

(strophe 2)

His mother, 'tis most like, burdened with many days, And whitened with old age, when she shall hear how frenzy

Has smitten his soul to ruin, Ailinon! ailinon! Will break forth her despair, not as the nightingale's Plaintive, tender lament, no, but in passion's wailing Shrill-toned cries; and with fierce strokes Wildly smiting her bosom, In grief's anguish her hands will rend her grey locks.

(antistrophe 2)

Yea, better Hell should hide one who is sick in soul, Though there be none than he sprung from a nobler lineage

Of the war-weary Greeks, yet Strayed from his inbred mood Now amidst alien thoughts dwells he a stranger. Hapless father! alas, bitter the tale that waits thee, Thy son's grievous affliction. No life save his alone Of Aeacid kings such a curse has ever haunted. (AJAX enters, carrying a sword. As he speaks, TECMESSA also enters.)

AJAX All things the long and countless lapse of time Brings forth. displays, then hides once more in gloom. Nought is too strange to look for; but the event May mock the sternest oath, the firmest will. Thus I, who late so strong, so stubborn seemed Like iron dipped, yet now grow soft with pity Before this woman, whom I am loath to leave Midst foes a widow with this orphaned child. But I will seek the meadows by the shore: There will I wash and purge these stains, if so I may appease Athena's heavy wrath. Then will I find some lonely place, where I May hide this sword, beyond all others cursed, Buried where none may see it, deep in earth. May night and Hades keep it there below. For from that hour my hand accepted it, The gift of Hector, deadliest of my foes, Nought from the Greeks towards me hath sped well. So now I find that ancient proverb true, Foes' gifts are no gifts: profit bring they none. Therefore henceforth I study to obey The Gods, and reverence the sons of Atreus. Our rulers are they: we must yield. How else? For to authority yield all things most dread And mighty. Thus must Winter's snowy feet Give place to Summer with her wealth of fruits; And from her weary round doth Night withdraw, That Day's white steeds may kindle heaven with light. After fierce tempest calm will ever lull The moaning sea; and Sleep, that masters all, Binds life awhile, yet loosens soon the bond. And who am I that I should not learn wisdom? Of all men I, whom proof hath taught of late How so far only should we hate our foes As though we soon might love them, and so far Do a friend service, as to one most like Some day to prove our foe; since oftenest men In friendship but a faithless haven find. Thus well am I resolved. (To TECMESSA) Thou, woman, pass

Within, and pray the gods that all things so May be accomplished as my heart desires. And you, friends, heed my wishes as she doth; And when he comes, bid Teucer he must guard My rights at need, and withal stand your friend. For now I go whither I needs must pass. Do as I bid. Soon haply you shall hear, With me, for all this misery, 'tis most well. (AJAX departs. TECMESSA goes into the tent.)

CHORUS (singing, strophe)

I thrill with rapture, flutter on wings of ecstasy. Io, Io, Pan, Pan! O Pan, Pan! from the stony ridge, Snow-bestrewn of Cyllene's height Appear roving across the waters, O dance-ordering king of gods, That thou mayst join me in flinging free Fancy measures of Nysa and of Cnossus. Yea for the dance I now am eager. And over the far Icarian billows come, O king Apollo, From Delos in haste, come thou, Thy kindly power here in our midst revealing.

(antistrophe)

Ares hath lifted horror and anguish from our eyes. Io, Io! Now again, Now, O Zeus, can the bright and blithe Glory of happier days return To our swift-voyaging ships, for now

Hath Ajax wholly forgot his grief, And all rites due to the gods he now Fain would meetly perform with loyal worship. Mighty is time to dwindle all things. Nought would I call too strange for belief, when Ajax thus beyond hope Hath learnt to repent his proud feuds, And lay aside anger against the Atreidae. (A MESSENGER enters.)

MESSENGER My friends, these tiding I would tell you first:

Teucer is present, from the Mysian heights But now returned, and in the central camp By all the Greeks at once is being reviled. As he drew near they knew him from afar, Then gathering around him one and all With taunts assailed him from this side and that, Calling him kinsman of that maniac, That plotter against the host, saying that nought Should save him; stoned and mangled he must die. And so they had come to such a pitch that swords Plucked from their sheaths stood naked in men's hands. Yet when the strife ran highest, it was stayed By words from the elders and so reconciled. But where is Ajax? I must speak with him. He whom it most concerns must be told all.

LEADER OF THE CHORUS He is not within, but has just now gone forth

With a new purpose yoked to a new mood.

MESSENGER Alas! Alas! Then too late on this errand was I sped By him who sent me; or I have proved too slow.

LEADER What urgent need has been neglected here?

MESSENGER Teucer forbade that Ajax should go forth Outside his hut, till he himself should come.

LEADER Well, he is gone. To wisest purpose now His mind is turned, to appease heaven's wrath.

MESSENGER These words of thine are filled with utter folly,

If there was truth in Calchas' prophecy.

LEADER What prophecy? And what know you of this thing?

MESSENGER Thus much I know, for by chance I was present.

Leaving the circle of consulting chiefs Where sat the Atreidae, Calchas went aside, And with kind purpose grasping Teucer's hand Enjoined him that by every artifice He should restrain Ajax within his tents This whole day, and not leave him to himself, If he wished ever to behold him alive. For on this day alone, such were his words, Would the wrath of divine Athena vex him. For the overweening and unprofitable Fall crushed by heaven-sent calamities (So the seer spoke), whene'er one born a man Has conceived thoughts too high for man's estate: And this man, when he first set forth from home, Showed himself foolish, when his father spoke to him Wisely: "My son, seek victory by the spear; But seek it always with the help of heaven." Then boastfully and witlessly he answered: "Father, with heaven's help a mere man of nought Might win victory: but I, albeit without Their aid, trust to achieve a victor's glory." Such was his proud vaunt. Then a second time Answering divine Athena, when she urged him To turn a slaughterous hand upon his foes, He gave voice to this dire, blasphemous boast: "Goddess, stand thou beside the other Greeks. Where I am stationed, no foe shall break through." By such words and such thoughts too great for man Did he provoke Athena's pitiless wrath. But if he lives through this one day, perchance, Should heaven be willing, we may save him yet. So spoke the seer; and Teucer from his seat No sooner risen, sent me with this mandate For you to observe. But if we have been forestalled, That man lives not, or Calchas is no prophet.

LEADER (calling) Woful Tecmessa, woman born to sorrow,

Come forth and hear this man who tells of a peril That grazes us too close for our mind's ease. (TECMESSA enters from the tent.)

TECMESSA Why alas do you break my rest again After brief respite from relentless woes?

LEADER Give hearing to this messenger, who brings Tidings that grieve me of how Ajax fares.

TECMESSA Ah me, what sayest thou, man? Are we undone?

MESSENGER I know not of thy fortune; but for Ajax, If he be gone abroad, my mind misgives.

TECMESSA Yes, he is gone. I am racked to know thy meaning.

MESSENGER Teucer commands you to keep him within doors,

And not to let him leave his tent alone.

TECMESSA And where is Teucer, and why speaks he thus?

MESSENGER He has but now returned, and he forebodes That this going-forth will prove fatal to Ajax.

TECMESSA Woe's me, alas! From whom has he learned this?

MESSENGER From the seer, Thestor's son, this very day, Which is fraught either with his death or life.

TECMESSA Ah me, my friends, avert this threatening doom

Speed some of you to hasten Teucer hither: Others go search the bays, some west, some east, And track my lord's ill-omened going-forth. Yes, now I know I have been deceived by him, And from his former favour quite cast out. Alas, child, what shall I do? Sit still I must not: But far as I have strength I too will go. Let us start quickly-'tis no time for loitering, If we would save one who is in haste to die.

LEADER I am ready, as not words alone shall prove, But speed of act and foot to make words good. (The CHORUS,

TECMESSA and MESSENGER go out. The scene changes to a lonely place by the sea-shore. Bushes and under- brush are in the background. AJAX enters alone.)

AJAX The slayer stands so that his edge may cleave Most surely (if there be leisure for such thought), Being the gift of Hector, of all friends Most unloved, and most hateful to my sight. Then it is planted in Troy's hostile soil, New-sharpened on the iron-biting whet. And heedfully have I planted it, that so With a swift death it prove to me most kind. Thus have I made all ready. Next be thou The first, O Zeus, to aid me, as is right. It is no mighty boon that I shall crave. Send some announcer of the evil news To Teucer, that he first may lift me up, When I have fallen upon this reeking sword, Lest ere he come some enemy should espy me And cast me forth to dogs and birds a prey. This, O Zeus, I entreat thee, and likewise call On Hermes, guide to the underworld, to lay me Asleep without a struggle, at one swift bound, When I have thrust my heart through with this sword. Next I call on those maidens ever-living And ever watchful of all human miseries, The dread swift-striding Erinyes, that they mark How by the Atreidae I have been destroyed: And these vile men by a vile doom utterly May they cut off, even as they see me here. Come, O ye swift avenging Erinyes, Spare not, touch with affliction the whole host. And thou, whose chariot mounts up the steep sky, Thou Sun, when on the land where I was born Thou shalt look down, check thy gold-spangled rein, And announce my disasters and my doom To my aged sire and her who nurtured me. She, woful woman, when she hears these tidings Will wail out a loud dirge through all the town. But I waste labour with this idle moan. The act must now be done, and that with speed. O Death, Death, come now and look upon me.- No, 'tis there I shall meet and speak to thee. But thee, bright daylight which I now behold, And Helios in his chariot I accost For this last time of all, and then no more. O sunlight! O thou hallowed soil, my own Salamis, stablished seat of my sire's hearth, And famous Athens, with thy kindred race, And you, ye springs and streams, and Trojan plains, Farewell, all ye who have sustained my life. This is the last word Ajax speaks to you.

All else in Hades to the dead will I say. (He falls on his sword. His body lies partially concealed by the underbrush. SEMI-CHORUS 1 enters.)

SEMI-CHORUS 1 (chanting) 'Tis toil on toil, and toil again.

Where! where! Where have not my footsteps been? And still no place reveals the secret of my search. But hark! There again I hear a sound. (SEMI-CHORUS 2 enters.)

SEMI-CHORUS 2 (chanting) 'Tis we, the ship-companions of your voyage.

SEMI-CHORUS 1 (chanting) Well how now?

SEMI-CHORUS 2 (chanting) We have searched the whole coast westward from the ship.

SEMI-CHORUS 1 (chanting) You have found nought?

SEMI-CHORUS 2 (chanting) A deal of toil, but nothing more to see.

SEMI-CHORUS 1 (chanting) Neither has he been found along the path

That leads from the eastern glances of the sun.

CHORUS (singing, strophe)

From whom, oh from whom? what hard son of the waves, Plying his weary task without thought of sleep, Or what Olympian nymph of hill or stream that flows Down to the Bosporus' shore, Might I have tidings of my lord Wandering somewhere seen Fierce of mood? Grievous it is When I have toiled so long, and ranged far and wide Thus to fail, thus to have sought in vain. Still the afflicted hero nowhere may I find. (TECMESSA enters and discovers the body.)

TECMESSA Alas, woe, woe!

CHORUS (chanting) Whose cry was it that broke from yonder copse?

TECMESSA Alas, woe is me!

LEADER OF THE CHORUS It is the hapless spear-won bride I see,

Tecmessa, steeped in that wail's agony.

TECMESSA I am lost, destroyed, made desolate, my friends.

LEADER What is it? Speak.

TECMESSA Ajax, our master, newly slaughtered lies Yonder, a hidden sword sheathed in his body.

CHORUS (chanting) Woe for my lost hopes of home! Woe's me, thou hast slain me, my king, Me thy shipmate, hapless man! Woful-souled woman too!

TECMESSA Since thus it is with him, 'tis mine to wail.

LEADER By whose hand has he wrought this luckless deed?

TECMESSA By his own hand, 'tis evident. This sword Whereon he fell, planted in earth, convicts him.

CHORUS (chanting) Woe for my blind folly! Lone in thy blood thou liest, from friends' help afar. And I the wholly witless, the all unwary, Forbore to watch thee. Where, where Lieth the fatally named, intractable Ajax?

TECMESSA None must behold him. I will shroud him wholly

In this enfolding mantle; for no man Who loved him could endure to see him thus Through nostrils and through red gash spouting up The darkened blood from his self-stricken wound. Ah me, what shall I do? What friend shall lift thee? Where is Teucer? Timely indeed would he now come, To compose duly his slain brother's corpse. O hapless Ajax, who wast once so great, Now even thy foes might dare to mourn thy fall.

CHORUS (chanting, antistrophe)

'Twas fate's will, alas, 'twas fate then for thou Stubborn of soul at length to work out a dark Doom of ineffable miseries. Such the dire Fury of passionate hate I heard thee utter fierce of mood Railing at Atreus' sons Night by night, day by day. Verily then it was the sequence of woes First began, when as the prize of worth Fatally was proclaimed the golden panoply.

TECMESSA Alas, woe, woe!

CHORUS (chanting) A loyal grief pierces thy heart, I know.

TECMESSA Alas, woe, woe!

CHORUS (chanting) Woman, I marvel not that thou shouldst wail

And wail again, reft of a friend so dear.

TECMESSA 'Tis thine to surmise, mine to feel, too surely.

CHORUS (chanting) 'Tis even so.

TECMESSA Ah, my child, to what bondage are we come, Seeing what cruel taskmasters will be ours.

CHORUS (chanting) Ah me, at what dost thou hint? What ruthless, unspeakable wrong From the Atreidae fearest thou? But may heaven avert that woe!

TECMESSA Ne'er had it come to this save by heaven's will.

CHORUS (chanting) Yes, too great to be borne this heaven-sent burden.

TECMESSA Yet such the woe which the dread child of Zeus,

Pallas, has gendered for Odysseus' sake.

CHORUS (chanting) Doubtless the much-enduring hero in his dark spy's soul exults mockingly, And laughs with mighty laughter at these agonies Of a frenzied spirit. Shame! Shame! Sharers in glee at the tale are the royal Atreidae.

TECMESSA Well, let them mock and glory in his ruin. Perchance, though while he lived they wished not for him,

They yet shall wail him dead, when the spear fails them.

Men of ill judgment oft ignore the good That lies within their hands, till they have lost it. More to their grief he died than to their joy, And to his own content. All his desire He now has won, that death for which he longed. Why then should they deride him? 'Tis the gods Must answer for his death, not these men, no. Then let Odysseus mock him with empty taunts. Ajax is no more with them; but has gone, Leaving to me despair and lamentation.

TEUCER (from without) Alas, woe, woe!

LEADER OF THE CHORUS Keep silence! Is it Teucer's voice I hear

Lifting a dirge over this tragic sight? (TEUCER enters.)

TEUCER O brother Ajax, to mine eyes most dear, Can it be thou hast fared as rumour tells?

LEADER Yes, he is dead, Teucer: of that be sure.

TEUCER Alas, how then can I endure my fate!

LEADER Since thus it is...

TEUCER O wretched, wretched me!

LEADER Thou hast cause to moan.

TEUCER O swift and cruel woe!

LEADER Too cruel, Teucer!

TEUCER Woe is me! But say- His child-where shall I find him? Tell me where.

LEADER Alone within the tent.

TEUCER (to TECMESSA) Then with all speed Go, bring him thither, lest some foe should snatch him Like a whelp from a lioness bereaved. Away! See it done quickly! All men are wont To insult over the dead, once they lie low. (TECMESSA departs.)

LEADER Yes, Teucer, while he lived, did he not charge thee

To guard his son from harm, as now thou dost?

TEUCER O sight most grievous to me of all sights That ever I have looked on with my eyes! And hatefullest of all paths to my soul This path that now has led me to thy side, O dearest Ajax, when I heard thy fate, While seeking thee I tracked thy footsteps out. For a swift rumour, as from some god, ran Through the Greek host that thou wast dead and gone. While yet far off I heard it, and groaned deep In anguish; now I see, and my life dies. Ay me! Uncover. Let me behold woe's very worst. (The cover is lifted from the body.) O ghastly sight! victim of ruthless courage!

What miseries hast thou dying sown for me! Whither, among what people, shall I go, Who in thy troubles failed to give thee succour? Oh doubtless Telamon, thy sire and mine, With kind and gracious face is like to greet me, Returned without thee: how else?-he who is wont Even at good news to smile none the sweeter. What will he keep back? What taunt not hurl forth Against the bastard of a spear-won slave, Him who through craven cowardice betrayed Thee, beloved Ajax- or by guile, that so I might inherit thy kingdom and thy house. So will he speak, a passionate man, grown peevish In old age, quick to wrath without a cause. Then shall I be cast off, a banished man, Proclaimed no more a freeman but a slave. Such is the home that waits me; while at Troy My foes are many, my well-wishers few. All this will be my portion through thy death. Ah me, what shall I do? How draw thee, brother, From this fell sword, on whose bright murderous point Thou hast breathed out thy soul? See how at last Hector, though dead, was fated to destroy thee! Consider, I pray, the doom of these two men. Hector, with that same

girdle Ajax gave him Was lashed fast to Achilles' chariot rail
And mangled till he had gasped forth his life. And 'twas from
him that Ajax had this gift, The blade by which he perished
and lies dead. Was it not some Erinys forged this sword,
And Hades the grim craftsman wrought that girdle? I at
least would maintain that the gods plan These things and
all things ever for mankind. But whosoever's judgment likes
not this, Let him uphold his doctrine as I mine.

LEADER Speak no more, but take counsel how to inter
Our dear lord, and what now it were best to say: For 'tis a
foe I see. Perchance he comes To mock our misery, villain
that he is.

TEUCER What chieftain of the host do you behold?

LEADER Menelaus, for whose sake we voyaged hither.

TEUCER 'Tis he. I know him well, now he is near.
(MENELAUS enters with his retinue.)

MENELAUS You, Sir, I warn you, raise not yonder corpse
For burial, but leave it as it lies.

TEUCER For what cause do you waste such swelling
words?

MENELAUS 'Tis my will, and his will who rules the
host.

TEUCER Let us know then what pretext you allege.

MENELAUS We hoped that we had brought this man
from home

To be a friend and champion for the Greeks: But a worse
than Phrygian foe on trial we found him. Devising death for
the whole host, by night He sallied forth against us, armed
for slaughter. And had not some god baffled this exploit,
Ours would have been the lot which now is his: While we
lay slain by a most shameful doom, He would have still been
living. But his outrage, Foiled by a god, has fallen on sheep
and herds. Wherefore there lives no man so powerful That

he shall lay this corpse beneath a tomb; But cast forth some-where upon the yellow sands It shall become food for the sea-shore birds. Then lift not up your voice in threatening fury. If while he lived we could not master him, Yet in death will we rule him, in your despite, Guiding him with our hands, since in his life At no time would he hearken to my words. Yet 'tis a sign of wickedness, when a subject Deigns not to obey those placed in power above him. For never can the laws be prosperously Stablished in cities where awe is not found; Nor may a camp be providently ruled Without the shield of dread and reverence. Yea, though a man be grown to mighty bulk, Let him look lest some slight mis-chance o'erthrow him. He with whom awe and reverence abide, Doubt not, will flourish in security. But where out-rage and licence are not checked, Be sure that state, though sped by prosperous winds, Some day at last will founder in deep seas. Yes, fear should be established in due season. Dream not that we can act as we desire, Yet avoid payment of the price in pain. Well, fortune goes by turns. This man was fiery And insolent once: 'tis mine now to exult. I charge thee, bury him not, lest by that act Thou thyself shouldst be digging thine own grave,

LEADER Menelaus, do not first lay down wise precepts, Then thyself offer outrage to the dead.

TEUCER (to the CHORUS) Never, friends, shall I mar-vel any more,

If one of low birth acts injuriously, When they who are accounted nobly born Can utter such injurious calum-nies. (To MENELAUS) Come, once more speak. You say you brought him hither? Took him to be a champion of the Greeks? Did he not sail as his own master, freely? How are you his chieftain? How have you the right To lord it o'er the folk he brought from home? As Sparta's lord you came, not as our master. In no way was it your prerogative To rule him, any more than he could you. As vassal of others you sailed hither, not As captain of us all, still less of Ajax. Go, rule those whom you may rule: chastise them With proud words. But this man, though you forbid me, Aye, and your fellow-captain, by just right Will I lay in his grave, scorning your threats. It was not for the sake of your lost wife He came to Troy, like your toil-broken serfs, But for the sake of oaths that he had sworn, Not for yours. What cared he for nobodies? Then come again and bring more heralds hither, And the captain of the host. For such as you I would not turn my head, for all your bluster.

LEADER Such speech I like not, either, in peril's midst:

For harsh words rankle, be they ne'er so just.

MENELAUS This bowman, it seems, has pride enough to spare.

TEUCER Yes, 'tis no mean craft I have made my own.

MENELAUS How big would be your boasts, had you a shield!

TEUCER Shieldless, I would outmatch you panoplied.

MENELAUS How terrible a courage dwells within your tongue!

TEUCER He may be bold of heart whose side right favours.

MENELAUS Is it right that my assassin should be honoured?

TEUCER Assassin? How strange, if, though slain, you live!

MENELAUS Heaven saved me: I was slain in his intent.

TEUCER Do not dishonour then the gods who saved you.

MENELAUS What, I rebel against the laws of heaven?
TEUCER, Yes, if you come to rob the dead of burial.

MENELAUS My own foes! How could I endure such wrong?

TEUCER Did Ajax ever confront you as your foe?

MENELAUS He loathed me, and I him, as well you know.

TEUCER Because to defraud him you intrigued for votes.

MENELAUS It was the judges cast him, and not I.

TEUCER Much secret villainy you could make seem fair.

MENELAUS That saying will bring someone into trouble.

TEUCER Not greater trouble than we mean to inflict.

MENELAUS My one last word: this man must not have burial.

TEUCER Then hear my answer: burial he shall have.

MENELAUS Once did I see a fellow bold of tongue, Who had urged a crew to sail in time of storm; Yet no voice had you found in him, when winds Began to blow; but hidden beneath his cloak The mariners might trample on him at will. And so with you and your fierce railleries, Perchance a great storm, though from a little cloud Its breath proceed, shall quench your blatant outcry.

TEUCER And I once saw a fellow filled with folly, Who gloried scornfully in his neighbour's woes. So it came to pass that someone like myself, And of like mood, beholding him spoke thus. "Man, act not wickedly towards the dead; Or, if thou dost, be sure that thou wilt rue it." Thus did he monish that infatuate man. And lo! yonder I see him; and as I think, He is none else but thou. Do I speak riddles?

MENELAUS I go. It were disgrace should any know I had fallen to chiding where I might chastise.

TEUCER Begone then. For to me 'twere worst disgrace That I should listen to a fool's idle blustering. (MENELAUS and his retinue depart.)

CHORUS (chanting) Soon mighty and fell will the strife be begun.

But speedily now, Teucer, I pray thee, Seek some fit place for his hollow grave, Which men's memories evermore shall praise, As he lies there mouldering at rest. (TECMESSA enters with EURYSACES.)

TEUCER Look yonder, where the child and wife of Ajax Are hastening hither in good time to tend The funeral rites of his unhappy corpse. My child, come hither. Stand near and lay thy hand As a suppliant on thy father who begat thee. And kneel imploringly with locks of hair Held in thy hand-mine, and hers, and last thine- The suppliant's treasure. But if any Greek By violence should tear thee from this corpse, For that crime from the land may he be cast Unburied, and his whole race from the root Cut off, even as I sever this lock. There, take it, boy, and keep it. Let none seek To move thee; but still kneel there and cling fast. And you, like men, no women, by his side Stand and defend him till I come again, When I have dug his grave, though all forbid. (TEUCER goes out.)

CHORUS (singing, strophe 1)

When will this agony draw to a close? When will it cease, the last of our years of exile? Years that bring me labour accurst of hurtling spears, Woe that hath no respite or end, But wide-spread over the plains of Troy Works sorrow and shame for Hellas' sons.

(antistrophe 1)

Would he had vanished away from the earth, Rapt to the skies, or sunk to devouring Hades, He who first revealed to the Greeks the use of arms Leagued in fierce confederate war! Ah, toils eternally breeding toils! Yea, he was the fiend who wrought man's ruin.

(strophe 2)

The wretch accurst, what were his gifts? Neither the
glad, festival wreath, Nor the divine, mirth-giving wine-cup;
No music of flutes, soothing and sweet: Slumber by night,
blissful and calm, None he bequeathed us. And love's joys,
alas! love did he banish from me. Here couching alone neglected, With hair by unceasing dews drenched evermore,
we curse Thy shores, O cruel Ilium.

(antistrophe 2)

Erewhile against terror by night, javelin or sword, firm
was our trust: He was our shield, valiant Ajax. But now a
malign demon of fate Claims him. Alas! When, when again
Shall joy befall me? Oh once more to stand, where on the
wooded headland The ocean is breaking, under The shadow
of Sunium's height; thence could I greet from far

The divine city of Athens. (TEUCER enters, followed by
AGAMEMNON and his retinue.)

TEUCER In haste I come; for the captain of the host, Agamemnon, I have seen hurrying hither. To a perverse tongue
now will he give rein.

AGAMEMNON Is it you, they tell me, have dared to
stretch your lips

In savage raillery against us, unpunished? 'Tis you I
mean, the captive woman's son. Verily of well-born mother
had you been bred, Superb had been your boasts and high
your strut, Since you, being nought, have championed one
who is nought,

Vowing that no authority is ours By sea or land to rule
the Greeks or you. Are not these monstrous taunts to hear
from slaves? What was this man whose praise you vaunt so
loudly? Whither went he, or where stood he, where I was
not? Among the Greeks are there no men but he? In evil
hour, it seems, did we proclaim The contest for Achilles' panoply, If come what may Teucer is to call us knaves, And if
you never will consent, though worsted, To accept the award
that seemed just to most judges, But either must keep pelt-

ing us with foul words, Or stab us craftily in your rage at losing. Where such discords are customary, never Could any law be stablished and maintained, If we should thrust the rightful winners by, And bring the rearmost to the foremost place. But such wrong must be checked. 'Tis not the big Broad-shouldered men on whom we most rely; No, 'tis the wise who are masters everywhere. An ox, however large of rib, may yet Be kept straight on the road by a little whip. And this corrective, I perceive, will soon Descend on you, unless you acquire some wisdom, Who, though this man is dead, a mere shade now, Can wag your insolent lips so freely and boldly. Come to your senses: think what you are by birth. Bring hither someone else, a man born free, Who in your stead may plead your cause before us. For when you speak, the sense escapes me quite: I comprehend not your barbarian tongue.

LEADER OF THE CHORUS Would that you both might learn wisdom and temperance.

There is no better counsel I can give you.

TEUCER Alas! how soon gratitude to the dead Proves treacherous and vanishes from men's minds, If for thee, Ajax, this man has no more The least word of remembrance, he for whom oft Toiling in battle thou didst risk thy life. But all that is forgotten and flung aside. Thou who but now wast uttering so much folly, Hast thou no memory left, how in that hour When, pent within your lines, you were already No more than men of nought, routed in battle, He alone stood forth to save you, while the flames Were blazing round the stern-decks of the ships Already, and while Hector, leaping high Across the trench, charged down upon the hulls? Who checked this ruin? Was it not he, who nowhere So much as stood beside thee, so thou sayest? Would you deny he acted nobly there? Or when again chosen by lot, unbidden, Alone in single combat he met Hector? For no runaway's lot did he cast in, No lump of clammy earth, but such that first It should leap lightly from the crested helm? His were these exploits; and beside him stood I the slave, the barbarian mother's son. Wretch, with what face can you fling forth

such taunts? Know you not that of old your father's father
Was Pelops, a barbarian, and a Phrygian? That your sire
Atreus set before his brother A feast most impious of his
own children's flesh? And from a Cretan mother you were
born, Whom when her father found her with a paramour,
He doomed her for dumb fishes to devour. Being such, do you
reproach me with my lineage? Telamon is the father who
begat me, Who, as the foremost champion of the Greeks,
Won as his bride my mother, a princes By birth, Laome-
don's daughter: a chosen spoil She had been given him by
Alcmena's son. Thus of two noble parents nobly born, How
should I shame one of my blood, whom now, Laid low by
such calamity, you would thrust Unburied forth, and feel no
shame to say it? But of this be sure: wheresoever you may
cast him, Us three also with him will you cast forth. For it
beseems me in his cause to die In sight of all, rather than for
the sake Of your wife-or your brother's should I say? Look
then not to my interest, but your own. For if you assail me,
you shall soon wish rather To have been a coward than too
bold against me. (ODYSSEUS enters.)

LEADER In good time, King Odysseus, hast thou come,
If 'tis thy purpose not to embroil but reconcile.

ODYSSEUS What is it, friends? Far off I heard high
words

From the Atreidae over this hero's corpse.

AGAMEMNON Royal Odysseus, but now from this man
We have been listening to most shameful taunts.

ODYSSEUS How shameful? I could find excuse for one
Who, when reviled, retorts with bitter words.

AGAMEMNON Yes, I repaid his vile deeds with revil-
ing.

ODYSSEUS What has he done thee whereby thou art
wronged?

AGAMEMNON He says he will not leave yon corpse un-
honoured

By sepulture, but will bury it in my spite.

ODYSSEUS May now a friend speak out the truth, yet still

As ever ply his oar in stroke with thine?

AGAMEMNON Speak: I should be witless else; for thee Of all the Greeks I count the greatest friend.

ODYSSEUS Then listen. For the gods' sake venture not Thus ruthlessly to cast forth this man unburied: And in no wise let violence compel thee To such deep hate that thou shouldst tread down justice.

Once for me too this man was my worst foe, From that hour when I won Achilles' arms; Yet, though he was such towards me, I would not so Repay him with dishonour as to deny That of all Greeks who came to Troy, no hero So valiant save Achilles have I seen. So it is not just thou shouldst dishonour him. Not him wouldst thou be wronging, but the laws Of heaven. It is not righteousness to outrage A brave man dead, not even though thou hate him.

AGAMEMNON Thou, Odysseus, champion him thus against me?

ODYSSEUS Yes; but I hated him while hate was honourable.

AGAMEMNON Shouldst thou not also trample on him when dead?

ODYSSEUS Atreides, glory not in dishonouring triumphs.

AGAMEMNON 'Tis hard for a king to act with piety.

ODYSSEUS Yet not hard to respect a friend's wise counsel.

AGAMEMNON A good man should obey those who bear rule.

ODYSSEUS Relent. 'Tis no defeat to yield to friends.

AGAMEMNON Reflect who it is to whom thou dost this grace.

ODYSSEUS This man was once my foe, yet was he noble.

AGAMEMNON Can it be thou wilt reverence a dead foe?

ODYSSEUS His worth with me far outweighs enmity.

AGAMEMNON Unstable of impulse are such men as thou.

ODYSSEUS Many are friends now and hereafter foes.

AGAMEMNON Do you then praise such friends as worth the winning?

ODYSSEUS I am not wont to praise a stubborn soul.

AGAMEMNON Cowards you would have us show ourselves this day.

ODYSSEUS Not so, but just men before all the Greeks.

AGAMEMNON You bid me then permit these funeral rites?

ODYSSEUS Even so: for I myself shall come to this.

AGAMEMNON Alike in all things each works for himself.

ODYSSEUS And for whom should I work, if not myself?

AGAMEMNON Let it be known then as your doing, not mine.

ODYSSEUS So be it. At least you will have acted nobly.

AGAMEMNON Nay, but of this be certain, that to thee Willingly would I grant a greater boon. Yet he, in that world as in this, shall be Most hateful to me. But act as you deem fit. (AGAMEMNON and his retinue go out.)

LEADER After such proof, Odysseus, a fool only Could say that inborn wisdom was not thine.

ODYSSEUS Let Teucer know that I shall be henceforth His friend, no less than I was once his foe. And I will join in burying this dead man, And share in all due rites, omitting none Which mortal men to noblest heroes owe.

TEUCER Noble Odysseus, for thy words I praise thee Without stint. Wholly hast thou belied my fears. Thou, his worst foe among the Greeks, hast yet Alone stood by him staunchly, nor thought fit To glory and exult over the dead, Like that chief crazed with arrogance, who came, He and his brother, hoping to cast forth The dead man shamefully without burial. May therefore the supreme Olympian Father, The remembering Fury and fulfilling Justice Destroy these vile men vilely, even as they Sought to cast forth this hero unjustly outraged. But pardon me, thou son of old Laertes, That I must scruple to allow thine aid In these rites, lest I so displease the dead. In all else share our toil; and wouldst thou bring Any man from the host, we grudge thee not. What else remains, I will provide. And know That thou towards us hast acted generously.

ODYSSEUS It was my wish. But if my help herein Pleases you not, so be it, I depart. (ODYSSEUS goes out.)

TEUCER 'Tis enough. Too long is the time we have wasted

In talk. Haste some with spades to the grave: Speedily hollow it. Some set the cauldron On high amid wreathing flames ready filled For pious ablution. Then a third band go, fetch forth from the tent All the armour he once wore under his shield. Thou too, child, lovingly lay thy hand On thy father's corpse, and with all thy strength Help me to lift him: for the dark blood-tide Still upward is streaming warm through the arteries. All then who openly now would appear Friends to the dead, come, hasten forwards. To our valiant lord this labour is due. We have served none nobler among men.

CHORUS (chanting) Unto him who has seen may manifold knowledge

Come; but before he sees, no man May divine what destiny awaits him.

THE END

The Women of Trachis

Dramatis Personae

DEIANEIRA
NURSE
HYLLUS, son of HERACLES and DEIANEIRA
MESSENGER
LICHAS, the herald of HERACLES
HERACLES
AN OLD MAN
CHORUS OF TRACHINIAN MAIDENS

At Trachis, before the house of HERACLES. Enter DEIANEIRA from the house, accompanied by the NURSE.

DEIANEIRA There is a saying among men, put forth of old, that thou canst not rightly judge whether a mortal's lot is good or evil, ere he die. But I, even before I have passed to the world of death, know well that my life is sorrowful and bitter; I, who in the house of my father Oeneus, while yet I dwelt at Pleuron, had such fear of bridals as never vexed any maiden of Aetolia. For my wooer was a river-god, Achelous, who in three shapes was ever asking me from my sire,- coming now as a bull in bodily form, now as serpent with sheeny coils, now with trunk of man and front of ox, while from a shaggy beard the streams of fountain-water flowed abroad. With the fear of such a suitor before mine eyes, I was always praying in my wretchedness that I might die, or ever I should come near to such a bed.

But at last, to my joy, came the glorious son of Zeus and Alcmena; who closed with him in combat, and delivered me.

How the fight was waged, I cannot clearly tell, I know not; if there be any one who watched that sight without terror, such might speak: I, as I sat there, was distraught with dread, lest beauty should bring me sorrow at the last. But finally the Zeus of battles ordained well,- if well indeed it be: for since I have been joined to Heracles as his chosen bride, fear after fear hath haunted me on his account; one night brings a trouble, and the next night, in turn, drives it out. And then children were born to us; whom he has seen only as the husbandman sees his distant field, which he visits at seedtime, and once again at harvest. Such was the life that kept him journeying to and fro, in the service of a certain master

But now, when he hath risen above those trials,- now it is that my anguish is sorest. Ever since he slew the valiant Iphitus, we have been dwelling here in Trachis, exiles from our home, and the guests of stranger; but where he is, no one knows; I only know that he is gone, and hath pierced my heart with cruel pangs for him. I am almost sure that some evil hath befallen him; it is no short space that hath passed, but ten long months, and then five more,- and still no message from him. Yes, there has been some dread mischance;- witness that tablet which he left with me ere he went forth: oft do I pray to the gods that I may not have received it for my sorrow.

NURSE Deianeira, my mistress, many a time have I marked thy bitter tears and lamentations, as thou bewailedst the going forth of Heracles; but now,- if it be meet to school the free-born with the counsels of a slave, and if I must say what behoves thee,- why, when thou art so rich in sons, dost thou send no one of them to seek thy lord;- Hyllus, before all, who might well go on that errand, if he cared that there should be tidings of his father's welfare? Lo! there he comes, speeding towards the house with timely step; if, then, thou deemest that I speak in season, thou canst use at once my counsel, and the man. (HYLLUS comes in from the side.)

DEIANEIRA My child, my son, wise words may fall, it seems, from humble lips; this woman is a slave, but hath spoken in the spirit of the free.

HYLLUS How, mother? Tell me, if it may be told.

DEIANEIRA It brings thee shame, she saith, that, when thy father hath been so long a stranger, thou hast not sought to learn where he is.

HYLLUS Nay, I know,- if rumour can be trusted.

DEIANEIRA And in what region, my child, doth rumour place him?

HYLLUS Last year, they say, through all the months, he toiled as bondman to Lydian woman.

DEIANEIRA If he bore that, then no tidings can surprise.

HYLLUS Well, he has been delivered from that, as I hear.

DEIANEIRA Where, then, is he reported to be now,- alive or dead?

HYLLUS He is waging or planning a war, they say, upon Euboea, the realm of Eurytus.

DEIANEIRA Knowest thou, my son, that he hath left with me sure oracles touching that land?

HYLLUS What are they, mother? I know not whereof thou speakest.

DEIANEIRA That either he shall meet his death, or, having achieved this task, shall have rest thenceforth, for all his days to come.

So, my child, when his fate is thus trembling in the scale, wilt thou not go to succour him? For we are saved, if he find safety, or we perish with him.

HYLLUS Ay, I will go, my mother; and, had I known the import of these prophecies, I had been there long since; but, as it was, my father's wonted fortune suffered me not to feel fear for him, or to be anxious overmuch. Now that I have the knowledge, I will spare no pains to learn the whole truth in this matter.

DEIANEIRA Go, then, my son; be the seeker ne'er so late, he is rewarded if he learn tidings of joy. (HYLLUS departs as the CHORUS OF TRACHINIAN MAIDENS enters. They are free-born young women of Trachis who are friends and confidantes of DEIANEIRA. She remains during their opening choral song.)

CHORUS (singing, strophe 1)

Thou whom Night brings forth at the moment when she is despoiled of her starry crown, and lays to rest in thy splendour, tell me, pray thee, O Sun-god, tell me where abides Alcmena's son? Thou glorious lord of flashing light, say, is he threading the straits of the sea, or hath he found an abode on either continent? Speak, thou who seest as none else can see!

(antistrophe 1)

For Deianeira, as I hear, hath ever an aching heart; she, the battle-prize of old, is now like some bird lorn of its mate; she can never lull her yearning, nor stay her tears; haunted by a sleepless fear for her absent lord, she pines on her anxious, widowed couch, miserable in her foreboding of mischance.

(strophe 2)

As one may see billow after billow driven over the wide deep by the tireless south-wind or the north, so the trouble of his life, stormy as the Cretan sea, now whirls back the son of Cadmus, now lifts him to honour. But some god ever saves him from the house of death, and suffers him not to fail.

(antistrophe 2)

Lady, I praise not this thy mood; with all reverence will I speak, yet in reproof. Thou dost not well, I say, to kill fair hope by fretting; remember that the son of Cronus himself, the all-disposing king, hath not appointed a painless lot for mortals. Sorrow and joy come round to all, as the Bear moves in his circling paths.

(epode)

Yea, starry night abides not with men, nor tribulation, nor wealth; in a moment it is gone from us, and another hath his turn of gladness, and of bereavement. So would I wish thee also, the Queen, to keep that prospect ever in thy thoughts; for when hath Zeus been found so careless of his children?

DEIANEIRA Ye have heard of my trouble, I think, and that hath brought you here; but the anguish which consumes my heart- ye are strangers to that; and never may ye learn it by suffering! Yes, the tender plant grows in those sheltered regions of its own! and the Sun-god's heat vexes it not, nor rain, nor any wind; but it rejoices in its sweet, untroubled being, til such time as the maiden is called a wife, and finds her portion of anxious thoughts in the night, brooding on danger to husband or to children. Such an one could understand the burden of my cares; she could judge them by her own.

Well, I have had many a sorrow to weep for ere now; but I am going to speak of one more grievous than them all.

When Heracles my lord was going from home on his last journey, he left in the house an ancient tablet, inscribed with tokens which he had never brought himself to explain to me before, many as were the ordeals to which he had gone forth. He had always departed as if to conquer, not to die. But now, as if he were a doomed man, he told me what portion of his substance I was to take for my dower, and how he would have his sons share their father's land amongst them. And he fixed the time; saying that, when a year and three months should have passed since he had left the country, then he was fated to die; or, if he should have survived that term, to live thenceforth an untroubled life.

Such, he said, was the doom ordained by the gods to be accomplished in the toils of Heracles; as the ancient oak at Dodona had spoken of yore, by the mouth of the two Peleiades. And this is the precise moment when the fulfilment of that word becomes due; so that I start up from sweet slumber, my friends, stricken with terror at the thought that I must remain widowed of the noblest among men.

LEADER OF THE CHORUS Hush- no more ill-omened words; I see a man approaching, who wears a wreath, as if for joyous tidings. (A MESSENGER enters.)

MESSENGER Queen Deianeira, I shall be the first of messengers to free thee from fear. Know that Alcmena's son lives and triumphs, and from battle brings the first-fruits to the gods of this land.

DEIANEIRA What news is this, old man, that thou hast told me?

MESSENGER That thy lord, admired of all, will soon come to thy house, restored to thee in his victorious might.

DEIANEIRA What citizen or stranger hath told thee this?

MESSENGER In the meadow, summer haunt of oxen, Lichas the herald is proclaiming it to many: from him I heard it, and flew hither, that I might be the first to give thee these tidings, and so might reap some guerdon from thee, and win thy grace.

DEIANEIRA And why is he not here, if he brings good news?

MESSENGER His task, lady, is no easy one; all the Malian folk have thronged around him with questions, and he cannot move forward: each and all are bent on learning what they desire, and will not release him until they are satisfied. Thus their eagerness detains him against his will; but thou shalt presently see him face to face.

DEIANEIRA O Zeus, who rulest the meads of Oeta, sacred from the scythe, at last, though late, thou hast given us joy! Uplift your voices, ye women within the house and ye beyond our gates, since now we are gladdened by the light of this message, that hath risen on us beyond my hope!

LEADER OF ONE SEMI-CHORUS (singing) Let the maidens raise a joyous strain for the house, with songs of triumph at the hearth; and, amidst them, let the shout of the men go up with one accord for Apollo of the bright quiver, our Defender! And at the same time, ye maidens, lift up a paean, cry aloud to his sister, the Ortygian Artemis, smiter of deer, goddess of the twofold torch, and to the Nymphs her neighbours!

LEADER OF OTHER SEMI-CHORUS My spirit soars; I will not reject the wooing of the flute.- O thou sovereign of my soul! Lo, the ivy's spell begins to work upon me! Euoe!- even now it moves me to whirl in the swift dance of Bachanals!

CHORUS Praise, praise unto the Healer!

LEADER OF WHOLE CHORUS See, dear lady, see! Behold, these tidings are taking shape before thy gaze.

DEIANEIRA I see it, dear maidens; my watching eyes had not failed to note yon company.   (Enter LICHAS, followed by Captive Maidens. Conspicuous among them is IOLE.) -All hail to the herald, whose coming hath been so long delayed!- if indeed thou bringest aught that can give joy.

LICHAS We are happy in our return, and happy in thy greeting, lady, which befits the deed achieved; for when a man hath fair fortune, he needs must win good welcome.

DEIANEIRA O best of friends, tell me first what first I would know,- shall I receive Heracles alive?

LICHAS I, certainly, left him alive and well,- in vigorous health, unburdened by disease.

DEIANEIRA Where, tell me- at home, or on foreign soil?

LICHAS There is a headland of Euboea, where to Cenaean Zeus he consecrates altars, and the tribute of fruitful ground.

DEIANEIRA In payment of a vow, or at the bidding of an

oracle?

LICHAS For a vow, made when he was seeking to conquer and despoil the country of these women who are before thee.

DEIANEIRA And these- who are they, I pray thee, and whose daughters? They deserve pity, unless their plight deceives me.

LICHAS These are captives whom he chose out for himself and for the gods, when he sacked the city of Eurytus.

DEIANEIRA Was it the war against that city which kept him away so long, beyond all forecast, past all count of days?

LICHAS Not so: the greater part of the time he was detained in Lydia,- no free man, as he declares, but sold into bondage. No offence should attend on the word, lady, when the deed is found to be of Zeus. So he passed a whole year, as he himself avows, in thraldom to Omphale the barbarian. And so stung was he by that reproach, he bound himself by a solemn oath that he would one day enslave, with wife and child, the man who had brought that calamity upon him. Nor did he speak the word in vain; but, when he bad been purged, gathered an alien host, and went against the city of Eurytus. That man, he said, alone of mortals, had a share in causing his misfortune. For when Heracles, an old friend, came to his house and hearth, Eurytus heaped on him the taunts of a bitter tongue and spiteful soul,- saying, 'Thou hast unerring arrows in thy hands, and yet my sons surpass thee in the trial of archery'; 'Thou art a slave,' he cried, 'a free man's broken thrall': and at a banquet, when his guest was full of wine, he thrust him from his doors.

Wroth thereat, when afterward Iphitus came to the hill of Tiryns, in search for horses that had strayed, Heracles seized a moment when the man's wandering thoughts went not with his wandering gaze, and hurled him from a tower-like summit. But in anger at that deed, Zeus our lord, Olympian sire of all, sent him forth into bondage, and spared not, because, this once, he had taken a life by guile. Had he wreaked his vengeance openly, Zeus would surely have pardoned him the righteous triumph; for the gods, too, love not insolence.

So those men, who waxed so proud with bitter speech, are themselves in the mansions of the dead, all of them, and their city is enslaved; while the women whom thou beholdest, fallen from happiness to misery, come here to thee; for such was thy lord's command, which I, his faithful servant, perform. He himself, thou mayest be sure,- so soon as he shall have offered holy sacrifice for his victory to Zeus from whom he sprang,- will be with thee. After all the fair tidings that have been told, this, indeed, is the sweetest word to hear.

LEADER OF THE CHORUS Now, O Queen, thy joy is assured; part is with thee, and thou hast promise of the rest.

DEIANEIRA Yea, have I not the fullest reason to rejoice at these tidings of my lord's happy fortune? To such fortune, such joy must needs respond. And yet a prudent mind can see room for misgiving lest he who prospers should one day suffer reverse. A strange pity hath come over me, friends, at the sight of these ill-fated exiles, homeless and fatherless in a foreign land; once the daughters, perchance, of free-born sires, but now doomed to the life of slaves. O Zeus, who turnest the tide of battle, never may I see child of mine thus visited by thy hand; nay, if such visitation is to be, may it not fall while Deianeira lives! Such dread do I feel, beholding these. (To IOLE) Ah, hapless girl, say, who art thou? A maiden, or a mother? To judge by thine aspect, an innocent maiden, and of a noble race. Lichas, whose daughter is this stranger? Who is her mother, who her sire? Speak, I pity her more than all the rest, when I behold her; as she alone shows due feeling for her plight.

LICHAS How should I know? Why should'st thou ask me? Perchance the off, spring of not the meanest in yonder land.

DEIANEIRA Can she be of royal race? Had Eurytus a daughter?

LICHAS I know not; indeed, I asked not many questions.

DEIANEIRA And thou hast not heard her name from any of her companions?

LICHAS No, indeed, I went through my task in silence.

DEIANEIRA Unhappy girl, let me, at least, hear it from thine own mouth. It is indeed distressing not to know thy name. (IOLE maintains her silence.)

LICHAS It will be unlike her former behaviour, then, I can tell thee, if she opens her lips: for she hath not uttered one word, but hath ever been travailing with the burden of her sorrow, and weeping bitterly, poor girl, since she left her wind-swept home. Such a state is grievous for herself, but claims our forbearance.

DEIANEIRA Then let her be left in peace, and pass under our roof as she wishes; her present woes must not be crowned with fresh pains at my hands; she hath enough already.-Now let us all go in, that thou mayest start speedily on thy journey, while I make all things ready in the house. (LICHAS leads the captives into the house. DEIANEIRA starts to follow them, but the MESSENGER, who has been present during the entire scene, detains her. He speaks as he moves nearer to her.)

MESSENGER Ay, but first tarry here a brief space, that thou mayest learn, apart from yonder folk, whom thou art taking to thy hearth, and mayest gain the needful knowledge of things which have not been told to thee. Of these I am in full possession.

DEIANEIRA What means this? Why wouldest thou stay my departure?

MESSENGER Pause and listen. My former story was worth thy hearing, and so will this one be, methinks.

DEIANEIRA Shall I call those others back? Or wilt thou speak before me and these maidens?

MESSENGER To thee and these I can speak freely; never mind the others.

DEIANEIRA Well, they are gone;- so thy story can proceed.

MESSENGER Yonder man was not speaking the straightforward truth in aught that he has just told. He has given false tidings now, or else his former report was dishonest.

DEIANEIRA How sayest thou? Explain thy whole drift clearly; thus far, thy words are riddles to me.

MESSENGER I heard this man declare, before many witnesses, that for this maiden's sake Heracles overthrew Eurytus and the proud towers of Oechalia; Love, alone of the gods, wrought on him to do those deeds of arms,- not the toilsome servitude to Omphale in Lydia, nor the death to which Iphitus was hurled. But now the herald has thrust Love out of sight, and tells different tale.

Well, when he could not persuade her sire to give him the maiden for his paramour, he devised some petty complaint as a pretext, and made war upon her land,- that in which, as he said, this Eurytus bore sway,- and slew the prince her father, and sacked her city. And now, as thou seest, he comes sending her to this house not in careless fashion, lady, nor like slave:-no, dream not of that,- it is not likely, if his heart is kindled with desire.

I resolved, therefore, O Queen, to tell thee all that I had heard from yonder man. Many others were listening to it, as I was, in the public place where the Trachinians were assembled; and they can convict him. If my words are unwelcome, I am grieved; but nevertheless I have spoken out the truth.

DEIANEIRA Ah me unhappy! In what plight do I stand? What secret bane have received beneath my roof? Hapless that I am! Is she nameless, then, as her convoy sware?

MESSENGER Nay, illustrious by name as by birth; she is the daughter of Eurytus, and was once called Iole; she of whose parentage Lichas could say nothing, because, forsooth, he asked no questions.

LEADER OF THE CHORUS Accursed, above other evil-doers, be the man whom deeds of treachery dishonour!

DEIANEIRA Ah, maidens, what am I to do? These latest tidings have bewildered me!

LEADER Go and inquire from Lichas; perchance he will tell the truth, if thou constrain him to answer.

DEIANEIRA Well, I will go; thy counsel is not amiss.

MESSENGER And I, shall I wait here? Or what is thy pleasure?

DEIANEIRA Remain;- here he comes from the house of his own accord, without summons from me. (Enter LICHAS)

LICHAS Lady, what message shall I bear to Heracles? Give me thy commands, for, as thou seest, I am going.

DEIANEIRA How hastily thou art rushing away, when thy visit had been so long delayed,- before we have had time for further talk.

LICHAS Nay, if there be aught that thou would'st ask, I am at thy service.

DEIANEIRA Wilt thou indeed give me the honest truth?

LICHAS Yes, be great Zeus my witness,- in anything that I know,

DEIANEIRA Who is the woman, then, whom thou hast brought?

LICHAS She is Euboean; but of what birth, I cannot say.

MESSENGER Sirrah, look at me:- to whom art thou speaking, think'st thou?

LICHAS And thou- what dost thou mean by such a question?

MESSENGER Deign to answer me, if thou comprehend-est.

LICHAS To the royal Deianeira, unless mine eyes deceive me,- daughter of Oeneus, wife of Heracles, and my queen.

MESSENGER The very word that I wished to hear from thee:- thou sayest that she is thy queen?

LICHAS Yes, as in duty bound.

MESSENGER Well, then, what art thou prepared to suf-fer, if found guilty of failing in that duty?

LICHAS Failing in duty? What dark saying is this?

MESSENGER 'Tis none; the darkest words are thine own.

LICHAS I will go, I was foolish to hear thee so long.

MESSENGER No, not till thou hast answered a brief question.

LICHAS Ask what thou wilt; thou art not taciturn.

MESSENGER That captive, whom thou hast brought home- thou knowest whom mean?

LICHAS Yes; but why dost thou ask?

MESSENGER Well, saidst thou not that thy prisoner-she, on whom thy gaze now turns so vacantly- was Iole, daughter of Eurytus?

LICHAS Said it to whom? Who and where is the man that will be thy witness to hearing this from me?

MESSENGER To many of our own folk thou saidst it: in the public gathering of Trachinians, a great crowd heard thus much from thee.

LICHAS Ay- said they heard-but 'tis one thing to report a fancy, and another to make the story good.

MESSENGER A fancy! Didst thou not say on thine oath that thou wast bringing her us a bride for Heracles?

LICHAS I? bringing a bride?- In the name of the gods, dear mistress, tell me who this stranger may be?

MESSENGER One who heard from thine own lips that the conquest of the whole city was due to love for this girl: the Lydian woman was not its destroyer, but the passion which this maid has kindled.

LICHAS Lady, let this fellow withdraw: to prate with the brainsick befits not sane man.

DEIANEIRA Nay, I implore thee by Zeus whose lightnings go forth over the high glens of Oeta, do not cheat me of the truth! For she to whom thou wilt speak is not ungenerous, nor hath she yet to learn that the human heart is inconstant to its joys. They are not wise, then, who stand forth to buffet against Love; for Love rules the gods as he will, and me; and why not another woman, such as I am? So I am mad indeed, if I blame my husband, because that distemper hath seized him; or this woman, his partner in a thing which is no shame to them, and no wrong to me. Impossible! No; if he taught thee to speak falsely, 'tis not a noble lesson that thou art learning; or if thou art thine own teacher in this, thou wilt be found cruel when it is thy wish to prove kind. Nay, tell me the whole truth. To a free-born man, the name of liar cleaves as a deadly brand. If thy hope is to escape detection, that, too, is vain; there are many to whom thou hast spoken, who will tell me.

And if thou art afraid, thy fear is mistaken. Not to learn the truth,-that, indeed, would pain me; but to know it- what is there terrible in that? Hath not Heracles wedded others ere now,- ay, more than living man,- and no one of them hath bad harsh word or taunt from me; nor shall this girl, though her whole being should be absorbed in her passion; for indeed I felt a profound pity when I beheld her, because her beauty hath wrecked her life, and she, hapless one, all innocent, hath brought her fatherland to ruin and to bondage.

Well, those things must go with wind and stream.- To thee I say,-deceive whom thou wilt, but ever speak the truth to me.

LEADER Hearken to her good counsel, and hereafter thou shalt have no cause to complain of this lady; our thanks, too, will be thine.

LICHAS Nay, then, dear mistress,- since I see that thou thinkest as mortals should think, and canst allow for weakness,- I will tell thee the whole truth, and hide it not. Yes, it is even as yon man saith. This girl inspired that overmastering love which long ago smote through the soul of Heracles; for this girl's sake the desolate Oechalia, her home, was made the prey of his spear. And he,- it is just to him to say so,- never denied this,- never told me to conceal it. But I, lady, fearing to wound thy heart by such tidings, have sinned, if thou count this in any sort a sin.

Now, however, that thou knowest the whole story, for both your sakes,- for his, and not less for thine own,- bear with the woman, and be content that the words which thou hast spoken regarding her should bind thee still. For he, whose strength is victorious in all else, hath been utterly vanquished by his passion for this girl.

DEIANEIRA Indeed, mine own thoughts move me to act thus. Trust me, I will not add a new affliction to my burdens by waging a fruitless fight against the gods.

But let us go into the house, that thou mayest receive my messages; and, since gifts should be meetly recompensed with gifts,- that thou mayest take these also. It is not right that thou shouldest go back with empty hands, after coming with such a goodly train. (Exit MESSENGER, as LICHAS and DEIANEIRA go into the house.)

CHORUS (singing, strophe)

Great and mighty is the victory which the Cyprian queen ever bears away. I stay not now to speak of the gods; I spare to tell how she beguiled the son of Cronus, and Hades, the lord of darkness, or Poseidon, shaker of the earth.

But, when this bride was to be won, who were the valiant rivals that entered the contest for her hand? Who went forth to the ordeal of battle, to the fierce blows and the blinding dust?

(antistrophe)

One was a mighty river-god, the dread form of a horned and four-legged bull, Achelous, from Oeniadae: the other came from Thebe, dear to Bacchus, with curved bow, and spears, and brandished club, the son of Zeus: who then met in combat, fain to win a bride: and the Cyprian goddess of nuptial joy was there with them, sole umpire of their strife.

(epode)

Then was there clatter of fists and clang of bow, and the noise of bull's horns therewith; then were there close-locked grapplings, and deadly blows from the forehead, and loud deep cries from both.

Meanwhile, she, in her delicate beauty, sat on the side of a hill that could be seen afar, awaiting the husband that should be hers.

So the battle rages, as I have told; but the fair bride who is the prize of the strife abides the end in piteous anguish. And suddenly she is parted from her mother, as when a heifer is taken from its dam. (DEIANEIRA enters from the house alone, carrying in her arms a casket containing a robe.)

DEIANEIRA Dear friends, while our visitor is saying his farewell to the captive girls in the house, I have stolen forth to you,- partly to tell you what these hands have devised, and partly to crave your sympathy with my sorrow.

A maiden,- or, methinks, no longer a maiden, but a mistress,- hath found her way into my house, as a freight comes to a mariner,- a merchandise to make shipwreck of my peace. And now we twain are to share the same marriage-bed, the same embrace. Such is the reward that Heracles hath sent me,- he whom I called true and loyal,- for guarding his home through all that weary time. I have no thought of anger against him, often as he is vexed with this distemper. But then to live with her, sharing the same union- what woman could endure it? For I see that the flower of her age is blossoming, while mine is fading; and the eyes of men love to cull the bloom of youth, but they turn aside from the old. This, then, is my fear,- lest Heracles, in name my spouse, should be the younger's mate.

But, as I said, anger ill beseems a woman of understanding. I will tell you, friends, the way by which I hope to find deliverance and relief. I had a gift, given to me long ago by a monster of olden time, aid stored in an urn of bronze; a gift which, while yet a girl, I took up from the shaggy-breasted Nessus,- from his life-blood, as he lay dying; Nessus, who used to carry men in his arms across the deep waters of the Evenus, using no oar to waft them, nor sail of ship.

I, too, was carried on his shoulders,- when, by my father's sending, first went forth with Heracles as his wife; and when I was in mid-stream, he touched me with wanton hands. I shrieked; the son of Zeus turned quickly round, and shot a feathered arrow; it whizzed through his breast to the lungs; and, in his mortal faintness, thus much the Centaur spake:-

'Child of aged Oeneus, thou shalt have at least this profit of my ferrying,- if thou wilt hearken,-because thou wast the last whom I conveyed. If thou gatherest with thy hands the blood clotted round my wound, at the place where the Hydra, Lerna's monstrous growth, hath tinged the arrow with black gall,- this shall be to thee a charm for the soul of Heracles, so that he shall never look upon any woman to love her more than thee.'

I bethought me of this, my friends- for, after his death, I had kept it carefully locked up in a secret place; and I have anointed this robe, doing everything to it as he enjoined while he lived. The work is finished. May deeds of wicked daring be ever far from my thoughts, and from my knowledge,- as I abhor the women who attempt them! But if in any wise I may prevail against this girl by love-spells and charms used on Heracles, the means to that end are ready;-unless, indeed, I seem to be acting rashly: if so, I will desist forthwith.

LEADER Nay, if these measures give any ground of confidence, we think that thy design is not amiss.

DEIANEIRA Well, the ground stands thus,- there is a fair promise; but I have not yet essayed the proof.

LEADER Nay, knowledge must come through action; thou canst have no test which is not fanciful, save by trial.

DEIANEIRA Well, we shall know presently:- for there I see the man already at the doors; and he will soon be going.- Only may my secret be well kept by you! While thy deeds are hidden, even though they be not seemly, thou wilt never be brought to shame. (LICHAS enters from the house.)

LICHAS What are thy commands? Give me my charge, daughter of Oeneus; for already I have tarried over long.

DEIANEIRA Indeed, I have just been seeing to this for thee, Lichas, while thou wast speaking to the stranger maidens in the house;- that thou shouldest take for me this long robe, woven by mine own hand, a gift to mine absent lord.

And when thou givest it, charge him that he, and no other, shall be the first to wear it; that it shall not be seen by the light of the sun, nor by the sacred precinct, nor by the fire at the hearth, until he stand forth, conspicuous before all eyes, and show it to the gods on a day when bulls are slain.

For thus had I vowed,- that if I should ever see or hear that he had come safely home, I would duly clothe him in this robe, and so present him to the gods, newly radiant at their altar in new garb.

As proof, thou shalt carry a token, which he will quickly recognise within the circle of this seal.

Now go thy way; and, first, remember the rule that messengers should not be meddlers; next, so bear thee that my thanks may be joined to his doubling the grace which thou shalt win.

LICHAS Nay, if I ply this herald-craft of Hermes with any sureness, I will never trip in doing thine errand: I will not fail to deliver this casket as it is, and to add thy words in attestation of thy gift.

DEIANEIRA Thou mayest be going now; for thou knowest well how things are with us in the house.

LICHAS I know, and will report, that all hath prospered.

DEIANEIRA And then thou hast seen the greeting given to the stranger maiden-thou knowest how I welcomed her?

LICHAS So that my heart was filled with wondering joy.

DEIANEIRA What more, then, is there for thee to tell? I am afraid that it would be too soon to speak of the longing on my part, before we know if I am longed for there. (LICHAS departs with the casket and DEIANEIRA retires into the house.)

CHORUS (Singing, strophe 1)

O ye who dwell by the warm springs between haven and crag, and by Oeta's heights; O dwellers by the land-locked waters of the Malian sea, on the shore sacred to the virgingoddess of the golden shafts, where the Greeks meet in famous council at the Gates;

(antistrophe 1)

Soon shall the glorious voice of the flute go up for you again, resounding with no harsh strain of grief, but with such music as the lyre maketh to the gods! For the son whom Alcmena bore to Zeus is hastening homeward, with the trophies of all prowess.

(strophe 2)

He was lost utterly to our land, a wanderer over sea, while

we waited through twelve long months, and knew nothing; and his loving wife, sad dweller with sad thoughts, was ever pining amid her tears. But now the War-god, roused to fury, hath delivered her from the days of her mourning.

(antistrophe 2)

May he come, may he come! Pause not the many-oared ship that carries him, till he shall have reached this town, leaving the island altar where, as rumour saith, he is sacrificing! Thence may he come, full of desire, steeped in love by the specious device of the robe, on which Persuasion hath spread her sovereign charm! (DEIANEIRA comes out of the house in agitation.)

DEIANEIRA Friends, how I fear that I may have gone too far in all that I have been doing just now!

LEADER What hath happened, Deianeira, daughter of Oeneus?

DEIANEIRA I know not; but feel a misgiving that I shall presently be found to have wrought a great mischief, the issue of a fair hope.

LEADER It is nothing, surely, that concerns thy gift to Heracles?

DEIANEIRA Yea, even so. And henceforth I would say to all, act not with zeal, if ye act without light.

LEADER Tell us the cause of thy fear, if it may be told.

DEIANEIRA A thing hath come to pass, my friends, such that, if I declare it, ye will hear a marvel whereof none could have dreamed.

That with which I was lately anointing the festal robe,- a white tuft of fleecy sheep's wool,- hath disappeared,- not consumed by anything in the house, but self-devoured and self-destroyed, as it crumbled down from the surface of a stone. But I must tell the story More at length, that thou mayest know exactly how this thing befell.

I neglected no part of the precepts which the savage Centaur gave me, when the bitter barb was rankling in his side: they were in my memory, like the graven words which no hand may wash from a tablet of bronze. Now these were his orders, and I obeyed them:-to keep this unguent in secret place, always remote from fire and from the sun's warm ray, until I should apply it, newly spread, where I wished. So had I done. And now, when the moment for action had come, I performed the anointing privily in the house, with a tuft of soft wool which I had plucked from a sheep of our home-flock; then I folded up my gift, and laid it, unvisited by sunlight, within its casket, as ye saw.

But as I was going back into the house, I beheld a thing too wondrous for words, and passing the wit of man to understand. I happened to have thrown the shred of wool, with which I bad been preparing the robe, into the full blaze of the sunshine. As it grew warm, it shrivelled all away, and quickly crumbled to powder on the ground, like nothing so much as the dust shed from a saw's teeth where men work timber. In such a state it lies as it fell. And from the earth, where it was strewn, clots of foam seethed up, as when the rich juice of the blue fruit from the vine of Bacchus is poured upon the ground.

So I know not, hapless one, whither to turn my thoughts; I only see that I have done a fearful deed. Why or wherefore should the monster, in his death-throes, have shown good will to me, on whose account he was dying? Impossible! No, he was cajoling me, in order to slay the man who had smitten him: and I gain the knowledge of this too late, when it avails no more. Yes, I alone- unless my foreboding prove false- I, wretched one, must destroy him! For I know that the arrow which made the wound did scathe even to the god Cheiron; and it kills all beasts that it touches. And since 'tis this same black venom in the blood that hath passed out through the wound of Nessus, must it not kill my lord also? I ween it must.

Howbeit, I am resolved that, if he is to fall, at the same time I also shall be swept from life; for no woman could bear to live with an evil name, if she rejoices that her nature is not evil.

LEADER Mischief must needs be feared; but it is not well to doom our hope before the event.

DEIANEIRA Unwise counsels leave no room even for a hope which can lend courage.

LEADER Yet towards those who have erred unwittingly, men's anger is softened; and so it should be towards thee.

DEIANEIRA Nay, such words are not for one who has borne a part in the ill deed, but only for him who has no trouble at his own door.

LEADER 'Twere well to refrain from further speech, unless thou would'st tell aught to thine own son; for he is at hand, who went erewhile to seek his sire. (Enter HYLLUS)

HYLLUS O mother, would that one of three things had befallen thee! Would that thou wert dead,- or, if living, no mother of mine,- or that some new and better spirit had passed into thy bosom.

DEIANEIRA Ah, my son, what cause have I given thee to abhor me?

HYLLUS I tell thee that thy husband- yea, my sire-bath been done to death by thee this day

DEIANEIRA Oh, what word hath passed thy lips, my child!

HYLLUS A word that shall not fail of fulfilment; for who may undo that which bath come to pass?

DEIANEIRA What saidst thou, my son? Who is thy warranty for charging me with a deed so terrible?

HYLLUS I have seen my father's grievous fate with mine own eyes; I speak not from hearsay.

DEIANEIRA And where didst thou find him,- where didst thou stand at his side?

HYLLUS If thou art to hear it, then must all be told. After sacking the famous town of Eurytus, he went his way with the trophies and first-fruits of victory. There is a sea-washed headland of Euboea, Cape Cenaeum, where he dedicated altars and a sacred grove to the Zeus of his fathers; and there I first beheld him, with the joy of yearning love.

He was about to celebrate a great sacrifice, when his own herald, Lichas, came to him from home, bearing thy gift, the deadly robe; which he put on, according to thy precept; and then began his offering with twelve bulls, free from blemish, the firstlings of the spoil; but altogether he brought a hundred victims, great or small, to the altar.

At first, hapless one, he prayed with serene soul, rejoicing in his comely garb. But when the blood-fed flame began to blaze from the holy offerings and from the resinous pine, a sweat broke forth upon his flesh, and the tunic clung to his sides, at every joint, close-glued, as if by a craftsman's hand; there came a biting pain that racked his bones; and then the venom, as of some deadly, cruel viper, began to devour him.

Thereupon he shouted for the unhappy Lichas,- in no wise to blame for thy crime,- asking what treason had moved him to bring that robe; but he, all-unknowing, hapless one, said that he had brought the gift from thee alone, as it had been sent. When his master heard it, as a piercing spasm clutched his lungs, he caught him by the foot, where the ankle turns in the socket, and hurled him at a surf-beaten rock in the sea; and he made the white brain to ooze from the hair, as the skull was dashed to splinters, and blood scattered therewith.

But all the people lifted up a cry of awe-struck grief, seeing that one was frenzied, and the other slain; and no one dared to come before the man. For the pain dragged him to earth, or made him leap into the air, with yells and shrieks, till the cliffs rang around, steep headlands of Locris, and Euboean capes.

But when he was spent with oft throwing himself on the

ground in his anguish, and oft making loud lament,- cursing his fatal marriage with thee, the vile one, and his alliance with Oeneus,- saying how he had found in it the ruin of his life,- then from out of the shrouding altar-smoke, he lifted up his wildly-rolling eyes, and saw me in the great crowd, weeping. He turned his gaze on me, and called me: 'O son, draw near; do not fly from my trouble, even though thou must share my death. Come, bear me forth, and set me, if thou canst, in a place where no man shall see me; or, if thy pity forbids that, at least convey me with all speed out of this land, and let me not die where I am.'

That command sufficed; we laid him in mid-ship, and brought him-but hardly brought him- to this shore, moaning in his torments. And ye shall presently behold him, alive, or lately dead.

Such, mother, are the designs and deeds against my sire whereof thou hast been found guilty. May avenging justice and the Erinys visit thee for them! Yes, if it be right, that is my prayer: and right it is,- for I have seen thee trample on the right, by slaying the noblest man in all the world, whose like thou shalt see nevermore! (DEIANEIRA moves towards the house.)

LEADER (to DEIANEIRA) Why dost thou depart in silence? Knowest thou not that such silence pleads for thine accuser? (DEIANEIRA goes in the house.)

HYLLUS Let her depart. A fair wind speed her far from my sight! Why should the name of mother bring her a semblance of respect, when she is all unlike a mother in her deeds? No, let her go,- farewell to her; and may such joy as she gives my sire become her own! (Exit HYLLUS, into the house.)

CHORUS (singing, strophe 1)

See, maidens, how suddenly the divine word of the old prophecy hath come upon us, which said that, when the twelfth year should have run through its full tale of months, it should end the series of toils for the true-born son of Zeus!

And that promise is wafted surely to its fulfilment. For how shall he who beholds not the light have toilsome servitude any more beyond the grave?

(antistrophe 1)

If a cloud of death is around him, and the doom wrought by the Centaur's craft is stinging his sides, where cleaves the venom which Thanatos begat and the gleaming serpent nourished, how can he look upon tomorrow's sun,- when that appalling Hydra-shape holds him in its grip, and those murderous goads, prepared by the wily words of black-haired Nessus, have started into fury, vexing him with tumultuous pain?

(strophe 2)

Of such things this hapless lady had no foreboding; but she saw great mischief swiftly coming on her home from the new marriage. Her own hand applied the remedy; but for the issues of a stranger's counsel, given at a fatal meeting,- for these, I ween, she makes despairing lament, shedding the tender dew of plenteous tears. And the coming fate foreshadows a great misfortune, contrived by guile.

(antistrophe 2)

Our streaming tears break forth: alas, a plague is upon him more piteous than any suffering that foemen ever brought upon that glorious hero.

Ah, thou dark steel of the spear foremost in battle, by whose might yonder bride was lately borne so swiftly from Oechalia's heights! But the Cyprian goddess, ministering in silence, hath been plainly proved the doer of these deeds.

LEADER OF ONE SEMI-CHORUS Is it fancy, or do I hear some cry of grief just passing through the house? What is this?

LEADER OF OTHER SEMI-CHORUS No uncertain sound, but a wail of anguish from within: the house hath some new trouble.

LEADER OF WHOLE CHORUS And mark how sadly, with what a cloud upon her brow, that aged woman approaches, to give us tidings. (Enter NURSE, from the house.)

NURSE Ah, my daughters, great, indeed, were the sorrows that we were to reap from the gift sent to Heracles!

LEADER Aged woman, what new mischance hast thou to tell?

NURSE Deianeira hath departed on the last of all her journeys, departed without stirring foot.

LEADER Thou speakest not of death?

NURSE My tale is told.

LEADER Dead, hapless one?

NURSE Again thou hearest it.

CHORUS Hapless, lost one! Say, what was the manner of her death?

NURSE Oh, a cruel deed was there!

CHORUS Speak, woman, how hath she met her doom?

NURSE By her own hand hath she died.

CHORUS What fury, what pangs of frenzy have cut her off by the edge of a dire weapon? How contrived she this death, following death,- all wrought by her alone?

NURSE By the stroke of the sword that makes sorrow.

CHORUS Sawest thou that violent deed, poor helpless one?

NURSE I saw it; yea, I was standing near.

CHORUS Whence came it? How was it done? Oh, speak

NURSE 'Twas the work of her own mind and her own hand.

CHORUS What dost thou tell us?

NURSE The sure truth.

CHORUS The first-born, the first-born of that new bride is a dread Erinys for this house!

NURSE Too true; and, hadst thou been an eye-witness of the action, verily thy pity would have been yet deeper.

LEADER And could a woman's hand dare to do such deeds?

NURSE Yea, with dread daring; thou shalt hear, and then thou wilt bear me witness.

When she came alone into the house, and saw her son preparing a deep litter in the court, that he might go back with it to meet his sire, then she hid herself where none might see; and, falling before the altars, she wailed aloud that they were left desolate; and, when she touched any household thing that she had been wont to use, poor lady, in the past, her tears would flow; or when, roaming hither and thither through the house, she beheld the form of any well-loved servant, she wept, hapless one, at that sight, crying aloud upon her own fate, and that of the household which would thenceforth be in the power of others.

But when she ceased from this, suddenly I beheld her rush into the chamber of Heracles. From a secret place of espial, I watched her; and saw her spreading coverings on the couch of her lord. When she had done this, she sprang thereon, and sat in the middle of the bed; her tears burst forth in burning streams, and thus she spake: 'Ah, bridal bed and bridal chamber mine, farewell now and for ever; never more shall ye receive me to rest upon this couch.' She said no more, but with a vehement hand loosed her robe, where the gold-wrought brooch lay above her breast, baring all her left side and arm. Then I ran with all my strength, and warned her son of her intent. But lo, in the space between my going and our return, she had driven a two-edged sword through her side to the heart.

At that sight, her son uttered a great cry; for he knew,

alas, that in his anger he had driven her to that deed; and he had learned, too late, from the servants in the house that she had acted without knowledge, by the prompting of the Centaur. And now the youth, in his misery, bewailed her with all passionate lament; he knelt, and showered kisses on her lips; he threw himself at her side upon the ground, bitterly crying that he had rashly smitten her with a slander,- weeping that he must now live bereaved of both alike,- of mother and of sire.

Such are the fortunes of this house. Rash indeed, is he who reckons on the morrow, or haply on days beyond it; for to-morrow is not, until to-day is safely past.

CHORUS (singing, strophe 1)

Which woe shall I bewail first, which misery is the greater? Alas, 'tis hard for me to tell.

(antistrophe 1)

One sorrow may be seen in the house; for one we wait with foreboding: and suspense hath a kinship with pain.

(strophe 2)

Oh that some strong breeze might come with wafting power unto our hearth, to bear me far from this land, lest I die of terror, when look but once upon the mighty son of Zeus!

For they say that he is approaching the house in torments from which there is no deliverance, a wonder of unutterable woe.

(antistrophe 2)

Ah, it was not far off, but close to us, that woe of which my lament gave warning, like the nightingale's piercing note!

Men of an alien race are coming yonder. And how, then, are they bringing him? In sorrow, as for some loved one, they move on their mournful, noiseless march.

Alas, he is brought in silence! What are we to think; that he is dead, or sleeping? (Enter HYLLUS and an OLD MAN, with attendants,bearing HERACLES upon a litter.)

HYLLUS Woe is me for thee, my father, woe is me for thee, wretched that I am! Whither shall I turn? What can I do? Ah me!

OLD MAN (whispering) Hush, my son! Rouse not the cruel pain that infuriates thy sire! He lives, though prostrated. Oh, put a stern restraint upon thy lips!

HYLLUS How sayest thou, old man- is he alive?

OLD MAN (whispering) Thou must not awake the slumberer! Thou must not rouse and revive the dread frenzy that visits him, my son!

HYLLUS Nay, I am crushed with this weight of misery- there is madness in my heart!

HERACLES (awaking) O Zeus, to what land have I come? Who are these among whom I lie, tortured with unending agonies? Wretched, wretched that I am! Oh, that dire pest is gnawing me once more!

OLD MAN (to HYLLUS) Knew I not how much better it was that thou shouldest keep silence, instead of scaring slumber from his brain and eyes?

HYLLUS Nay, I cannot be patient when I behold this misery.

HERACLES O thou Cenaean rock whereon mine altars rose, what a cruel reward hast thou won me for those fair offerings,- be Zeus my witness! Ah, to what ruin hast thou brought me, to what ruin! Would that I had never beheld thee for thy sorrow! Then had I never come face to face with this fiery madness, which no spell can soothe! Where is the charmer, where is the cunning healer, save Zeus alone, that shall lull this plague to rest? I should marvel, if he ever came within my ken!

(strophe 1)

Ah! Leave me, hapless one, to my rest- leave me to my last rest!

(strophe 2)

Where art thou touching me? Whither wouldst thou turn me? Thou wilt kill me, thou wilt kill me! If there be any pang that slumbers, thou hast aroused it!

It hath seized me,- oh, the pest comes again!- Whence are ye, most ungrateful of all the Greeks? I wore out my troublous days in ridding Greece of pests, on the deep and in all forests; and now, when I am stricken, will no man succour me with merciful fire of sword?

(antistrophe 1)

Oh, will no one come and sever the head, at one fierce stroke, from this wretched body? Woe, woe is me!

OLD MAN Son of Heracles, this task exceeds my strength,- help thou,- for strength is at thy command, too largely to need my aid in his relief.

HYLLUS My hands are helping; but no resource, in myself or from another, avails me to make his life forget its anguish:- such is the doom appointed by Zeus!

HERACLES (strophe 3)

O my son, where art thou? Raise me,- take hold of me,- thus thus! Alas, my destiny!

(antistrophe 2)

Again, again the cruel pest leaps forth to rend me, the fierce plague with which none may cope!

O Pallas, Pallas, it tortures me again! Alas, my son, pity thy sire,- draw a blameless sword, and smite beneath my collar-bone, and heal this pain wherewith thy godless mother hath made me wild! So may I see her fall,- thus, even thus, as she hath destroyed me!

(antistrophe 3)

Sweet Hades, brother of Zeus, give me rest, give me rest,- end my woe by a swiftly-sped doom!

LEADER OF THE CHORUS I shudder, friends, to hear these sorrows of our lord; what a man is here, and what torments afflict him!

HERACLES Ah, fierce full oft, and grievous not in name alone, have been the labours of these hands, the burdens borne upon these shoulders! But no toil ever laid on me by the wife of Zeus or by the hateful Eurystheus was like unto this thing which the daughter of Oeneus, fair and false, hath fastened upon my back,- this woven net of the Furies, in which I perish! Glued to my sides, it hath eaten my flesh to the inmost parts; it is ever with me, sucking the channels of my breath; already it hath drained my fresh lifeblood, and my whole body is wasted, a captive to these unutterable bonds.

Not the warrior on the battle-field, not the Giants' earth-born host, nor the might of savage beasts, hath ever done unto me thus,- not Hellas, nor the land of the alien, nor any land to which I have come as a deliverer: no, a woman, a weak woman, born not to the strength of man, all alone hath vanquished me, without stroke of sword

Son, show thyself my son indeed, and do not honour a mother's name above a sire's: bring forth the woman that bare thee, and give her with thine own hands into my hand, that I may know of a truth which sight grieves thee most,- my tortured frame, or hers, when she suffers her righteous doom!

Go, my son, shrink not- and show thy pity for me, whom many might deem pitiful,- for me, moaning and weeping like a girl;- and the man lives not who can say that he ever saw me do thus before; no, without complaining I still went whither mine evil fortune led. But now, alas, the strong man hath been found a woman.

Approach, stand near thy sire, and see what a fate it

is that hath brought me to this pass; for I will lift the veil. Behold! Look, all of you, on this miserable body; see how wretched, how piteous is my plight!

Ah, woe is me! The burning throe of torment is there anew, it darts through my sides- I must wrestle once more with that cruel, devouring plague!

O thou lord of the dark realm, receive me! Smite me, O fire of Zeus! Hurl down thy thunderbolt, O King, send it, O father, upon my head! For again the pest is consuming me; it hath blazed forth, it hath started into fury! O hands, my hands, O shoulders and breast and trusty arms, ye, now in this plight, are the same whose force of old subdued the dweller in Nemea, the scourge of herdsmen, the lion, a creature that no man might approach or confront; ye tamed the Lernaean Hydra, and that monstrous host of double form, man joined to steed, a race with whom none may commune, violent, lawless, of surpassing might; ye tamed the Erymanthian beast, and the three-headed whelp of Hades underground, a resistless terror, offspring of the dread Echidna; ye tamed the dragon that guarded the golden fruit in the utmost places of the earth.

These toils and countless others have I proved, nor hath any man vaunted a triumph over my prowess. But now, with joints unhinged and with flesh torn to shreds, I have become the miserable prey of an unseen destroyer,- I, who am called the son of noblest mother,- I, whose reputed sire is Zeus, lord of the starry sky.

But ye may be sure of one thing:- though I am as nought, though I cannot move a step, yet she who hath done this deed shall feel my heavy hand even now: let her but come, and she shall learn to proclaim this message unto all, that in my death, as in my life, I chastised the wicked!

LEADER Ah, hapless Greece, what mourning do I forsee for her, if she must lose this man

HYLLUS Father, since thy pause permits an answer, hear me, afflicted though thou art. I will ask thee for no more than is my due. Accept my counsels, in a calmer mood than that to which this anger stings thee: else thou canst not learn how vain is thy desire for vengeance, and how causeless thy resentment.

HERACLES Say what thou wilt, and cease; in this my pain I understand nought of all thy riddling words.

HYLLUS I come to tell thee of my mother,- how it is now with her, and how she sinned unwittingly.

HERACLES Villain! What- hast thou dared to breathe her name again in my hearing,- the name of the mother who hath slain thy sire?

HYLLUS Yea, such is her state that silence is unmeet.

HERACLES Unmeet, truly, in view of her past crimes.

HYLLUS And also of her deeds this day,- as thou wilt own.

HERACLES Speak,- but give heed that thou be not found a traitor.

HYLLUS These are my tidings. She is dead, lately slain.

HERACLES By whose hand? A wondrous message, from a prophet of ill-omened voice!

HYLLUS By her own hand, and no stranger's.

HERACLES Alas, ere she died by mine, as she deserved!

HYLLUS Even thy wrath would be turned, couldst thou hear all.

HERACLES A strange preamble; but unfold thy meaning.

HYLLUS The sum is this;- she erred, with a good intent.

HERACLES Is it a good deed, thou wretch, to have slain thy sire?

HYLLUS Nay, she thought to use a love-charm for thy

heart, when she saw the new bride in the house; but missed her aim.

HERACLES And what Trachinian deals in spells so potent?

HYLLUS Nessus the Centaur persuaded her of old to inflame thy desire with such a charm.

HERACLES Alas, alas, miserable that I am! Woe is me, I am lost,- undone, undone! No more for me the light of day! Alas, now I see in what a plight stand! Go, my son,- for thy father's end hath come,- summon, I pray thee, all thy brethren; summon, too, the hapless Alcmena, in vain the bride of Zeus,- that ye may learn from my dying lips what oracles know.

HYLLUS Nay, thy mother is not here; as it chances, she hath her abode at Tiryns by the sea. Some of thy children she hath taken to live with her there, and others, thou wilt find, are dwelling in Thebe's town. But we who are with thee, my father, will render all service that is needed, at thy bidding.

HERACLES Hear, then, thy task: now is the time to show what stuff is in thee, who art called my son.

It was foreshown to me by my Sire of old that I should perish by no creature that had the breath of life, but by one that had passed to dwell with Hades. So I have been slain by this savage Centaur, the living by the dead, even as the divine will had been foretold.

And I will show thee how later oracles tally therewith, confirming the old prophecy. I wrote them down in the grove of the Selli, dwellers on the hills, whose couch is on the ground; they were given by my Father's oak of many tongues; which said that, at the time which liveth and now is, my release from the toils laid upon me should be accomplished. And I looked for prosperous days; but the meaning, it seems, was only that should die; for toil comes no more to the dead.

Since, then, my son, those words are clearly finding their fulfilment, thou, on thy part, must lend me thine aid. Thou must not delay, and so provoke me to bitter speech: thou must consent and help with a good grace, as one who hath learned that best of laws, obedience to a sire.

HYLLUS Yea, father,- though I fear the issue to which our talk hath brought me,- I will do thy good pleasure.

HERACLES First of all, lay thy right hand in mine.

HYLLUS For what purpose dost thou insist upon his pledge?

HERACLES Give thy hand at once- disobey me not!

HYLLUS Lo, there it is: thou shalt not be gainsaid.

HERACLES Now, swear by the head of Zeus my sire!

HYLLUS To do what deed? May this also be told?

HERACLES To perform for me the task that I shall enjoin.

HYLLUS I swear it, with Zeus for witness of the oath.

HERACLES And pray that, if thou break this oath, thou mayest suffer.

HYLLUS I shall not suffer, for I shall keep it:- yet so I pray.

HERACLES Well, thou knowest the summit of Oeta, sacred to Zeus?

HYLLUS Ay; I have often stood at his altar on that height.

HERACLES Thither, then, thou must carry me up with thine own hands, aided by what friends thou wilt; thou shalt lop many a branch from the deep-rooted oak, and hew many a faggot also from the sturdy stock of the wild-olive; thou shalt lay my body thereupon, and kindle it with flaming pine-torch.

And let no tear of mourning be seen there; no, do this

without lament and without weeping, if thou art indeed my son. But if thou do it not, even from the world below my curse and my wrath shall wait on thee for ever.

HYLLUS Alas, my father, what hast thou spoken? How hast thou dealt with me!

HERACLES I have spoken that which thou must perform; if thou wilt not, then get thee some other sire, and be called my son no more!

HYLLUS Woe, woe is me! What a deed dost thou require of me, my father,-that I should become thy murderer, guilty of thy blood!

HERACLES Not so, in truth, but healer of my sufferings, sole physician of my pain!

HYLLUS And how, by enkindling thy body, shall I heal it?

HERACLES Nay, if that thought dismay thee, at least perform the rest.

HYLLUS The service of carrying thee shall not be refused.

HERACLES And the heaping of the pyre, as I have bidden?

HYLLUS Yea, save that I will not touch it with mine own hand. All else will I do, and thou shalt have no hindrance on my part.

HERACLES Well, so much shall be enough.- But add one small boon to thy large benefits.

HYLLUS Be the boon never so large, it shall be granted.

HERACLES Knowest thou, then, the girl whose sire was Eurytus?

HYLLUS It is of Iole that thou speakest, if I mistake not.

HERACLES Even so. This, in brief, is the charge that I give thee, my son. When am dead, if thou wouldest show a pious remembrance of thine oath unto thy father, disobey me not, but take this woman to be thy wife. Let no other espouse her who hath lain at my side, but do thou, O my son, make that marriage-bond thine own. Consent: after loyalty in great matters, to rebel in less is to cancel the grace that bad been won.

HYLLUS Ah me, it is not well to be angry with a sick man: but who could bear to see him in such a mind?

HERACLES Thy words show no desire to do my bidding.

HYLLUS What! When she alone is to blame for my mother's death, and for thy present plight besides? Lives there the man who would make such choice, unless he were maddened by avenging fiends?

Better were it, father, that I too should die, rather than live united to the worst of our foes!

HERACLES He will render no reverence, it seems, to my dying prayer.- Nay, be sure that the curse of the gods will attend thee for disobedience to my voice.

HYLLUS Ah, thou wilt soon show, methinks, how distempered thou art!

HERACLES Yea, for thou art breaking the slumber of my plague.

HYLLUS Hapless that I am! What perplexities surround me!

HERACLES Yea, since thou deignest not to hear thy sire.

HYLLUS But must I learn, then, to be impious, my father?

HERACLES 'Tis not impiety, if thou shalt gladden my heart.

HYLLUS Dost thou command me, then, to do this deed, as a clear duty?

HERACLES I command thee,- the gods bear me witness!

HYLLUS Then will I do it, and refuse not,- calling upon the gods to witness thy deed. I can never be condemned for loyalty to thee, my father.

HERACLES Thou endest well; and to these words, my son, quickly add the gracious deed, that thou mayest lay me on the pyre before any pain returns to rend or sting me.

Come, make haste and lift me! This, in truth, is rest from troubles; this is the end, the last end, of Heracles!

HYLLUS Nothing, indeed, hinders the fulfilment of thy wish, since thy command constrains us, my father.

HERACLES (chanting) Come, then, ere thou arouse this plague, O my stubborn soul, give me a curb as of steel on lips set like stone to stone, and let no cry escape them; seeing that the deed which thou art to do, though done perforce, is yet worthy of thy joy!

HYLLUS (chanting) Lift him, followers! And grant me full forgiveness for this; but mark the great cruelty of the gods in the deeds that are being done. They beget children, they are hailed as fathers, and yet they can look upon such sufferings. (The attendants raise HERACLES on the litter and move slowly off, as HYLLUS chants to the CHORUS in the closing lines.) No man foresees the future; but the present is fraught with mourning for us, and with shame for the powers above, and verily with anguish beyond compare for him who endures this doom.

Maidens, come ye also, nor linger at the house; ye who have lately seen a dread death, with sorrows manifold and strange: and in all this there is nought but Zeus.

THE END

Electra

Dramatis Personae

ORESTES, son of Agamemnon and CLYTEMNESTRA
ELECTRA, sister of ORESTES
CHRYSOTHEMIS, sister of ORESTES
AN OLD MAN, formerly the PAEDAGOGUS or Attendant Of
ORESTES
CLYTEMNESTRA
AEGISTHUS
CHORUS OF WOMEN OF MYCENAE
Mute Persons
PYLADES, son of Strophius, King of Crisa, the friend Of
ORESTES.
A handmaid of CLYTEMNESTRA. Two attendants of OR-
ESTES

At Mycenae, before the palace of the Pelopidae. It is morning and the new-risen sun is bright. The PAEDAGO-GUS enters on the left of the spectators, accompanied by the two youths, ORESTES and PYLADES.

PAEDAGOGUS Son of him who led our hosts at Troy of old, son of Agamemnon!- now thou mayest behold with thine eyes all that thy soul hath desired so long. There is the ancient Argos of thy yearning,- that hallowed scene whence the gadfly drove the daughter of Inachus; and there, Orestes, is the Lycean Agora, named from the wolf-slaying god; there, on the left, Hera's famous temple; and in this place to which we have come, deem that thou seest Mycenae rich in gold, with the house of the Pelopidae there, so often stained with bloodshed; whence I carried thee of yore, from the slaying of thy father, as thy kinswoman, thy sister, charged me; and saved thee, and reared thee up to manhood, to be the avenger of thy murdered sire.

Now, therefore, Orestes, and thou, best of friends, Pylades, our plans must be laid quickly; for lo, already the sun's bright ray is waking the songs of the birds into clearness, and the dark night of stars is spent. Before, then, anyone comes forth from the house, take counsel; seeing that the time allows not of delay, but is full ripe for deeds.

ORESTES True friend and follower, how well dost thou prove thy loyalty to our house! As a steed of generous race, though old, loses not courage in danger, but pricks his ear, even so thou urgest us forward, and art foremost in our support. I will tell thee, then, what I have determined; listen closely to my words, and correct me, if I miss the mark in aught.

When I went to the Pythian oracle, to learn how I might avenge my father on his murderers, Phoebus gave me the response which thou art now to hear:- that alone, and by stealth, without aid of arms or numbers, I should snatch the righteous vengeance of my hand. Since, then, the god spake to us on this wise, thou must go into yonder house, when opportunity gives thee entrance, and learn all that is passing there, so that thou mayest report to us from sure knowledge. Thine age, and the lapse of time, will prevent them from recognising thee; they will never suspect who thou art, with that silvered hair. Let thy tale be that thou art a Phocian stranger, sent by Phanoteus; for he is the greatest of their allies. Tell them, and confirm it with thine oath, that Orestes hath perished by a fatal chance,- hurled at the Pythian games from his rapid chariot; be that the substance of thy story.

We, meanwhile, will first crown my father's tomb, as the god enjoined, with drink-offerings and the luxuriant tribute of severed hair; then come back, bearing in our hands an urn of shapely bronze,-now hidden in the brushwood, as I think thou knowest,- so to gladden them with the false tidings that this my body is no more, but has been consumed with fire and turned to ashes. Why should the omen trouble me, when by a feigned death I find life indeed, and win renown? I trow, no word is ill-omened, if fraught with gain. Often ere now have I seen wise men die in vain report; then, when they return home, they are held in more abiding honour: as I trust that from this rumour I also shall emerge in radiant life, and yet shine like a star upon my foes.

O my fatherland, and ye gods of the land, receive me with good fortune in this journey,- and ye also, halls of my fathers, for I come with divine mandate to cleanse you righteously; send me not dishonoured from the land, but grant that I may rule over my possessions, and restore my house!

Enough;- be it now thy care, old man, to go and heed thy task; and we twain will go forth; for so occasion bids, chief ruler of every enterprise for men.

ELECTRA (within) Ah me, ah me!

PAEDAGOGUS Hark, my son,- from the doors, methought, came the sound of some handmaid moaning within.

ORESTES Can it be the hapless Electra? Shall we stay here, and listen to her laments?

PAEDAGOGUS No, no: before all else, let us seek to obey the command of Loxias, and thence make a fair beginning, by pouring libations to thy sire; that brings victory within our grasp, and gives us the mastery in all that we do. (Exeunt PAEDAGOGUS on the spectators' left, ORESTES and PYLADES the right.- Enter ELECTRA, from the house. She is meanly clad.)

ELECTRA (chanting, systema)

O thou pure sunlight, and thou air, earth's canopy, how

often have ye heard the strains of my lament, the wild blows dealt against this bleeding breast, when dark night fails! And my wretched couch in yonder house of woe knows well, ere now, how I keep the watches of the night,- how often I bewail my hapless sire; to whom deadly Ares gave not of his gifts in a strange land, but my mother, and her mate Aegisthus, cleft his head with murderous axe, as woodmen fell an oak. And for this no plaint bursts from any lip save mine, when thou, my father, hath died a death so cruel and so piteous!

(antisystema)

But never will I cease from dirge and sore lament, while I look on the trembling rays of the bright stars, or on this light of day; but like the nightingale, slayer of her offspring, I will wail without ceasing, and cry aloud to all, here, at the doors of my father.

O home of Hades and Persephone! O Hermes of the shades! potent Curse, and ye, dread daughters of the gods, Erinyes,- Ye who behold when a life is reft by violence, when a bed is dishonoured by stealth,- come, help me, avenge the murder of my sire,- and send to me my brother; for I have no more the strength to bear up alone against the load of grief that weighs me down. (As ELECTRA finishes her lament, (the CHORUS OF WOMEN OF MYCENAE enter. The following) lines between ELECTRA and the CHORUS are chanted responsively.)

CHORUS (strophe 1)

Ah, Electra, child of a wretched mother, why art thou ever pining thus in ceaseless lament for Agamemnon, who long ago was wickedly ensnared by thy false mother's wiles, and betrayed to death by dastardly hand? Perish the author of that deed, if I may utter such prayer!

ELECTRA Ah, noble-hearted maidens, ye have come to soothe my woes. I know and feel it, it escapes me not; but I cannot leave this task undone, or cease from mourning for my hapless sire. Ah, friends whose love responds to mine in every mood, leave me to rave thus,- Oh leave me, I entreat you!

CHORUS (antistrophe 1)

But never by laments or prayers shalt thou recall thy sire from that lake of Hades to which all must pass. Nay, thine is a fatal course of grief, passing ever from due bounds into a cureless sorrow; wherein there is no deliverance from evils. Say, wherefore art thou enamoured of misery?

ELECTRA Foolish is the child who forgets a parent's piteous death. No, dearer to my soul is the mourner that laments for Itys, Itys, evermore, that bird distraught with grief, the messenger of Zeus. Ah, queen of sorrow, Niobe, thee I deem divine,- thee, who evermore weepest in thy rocky tomb!

CHORUS (strophe 2)

Not to thee alone of mortals, my daughter, hath come any sorrow which thou bearest less calmly than those within, thy kinswomen and sisters, Chrysothemis and Iphianassa,I who still live,- as he, too, lives, sorrowing in a secluded youth, yet happy in that this famous realm of Mycenae shall one day welcome him to his heritage, when the kindly guidance of Zeus shall have brought him to this land, Orestes.

ELECTRA Yes, I wait for him with unwearied longing, as I move on my sad path from day to day, unwed and childless, bathed in tears, bearing that endless doom of woe; but he forgets all that he has suffered and heard. What message comes to me, that is not belied? He is ever yearning to be with us, but, though he yearns, he never resolves.

CHORUS (antistrophe 2)

Courage, my daughter, courage; great still in heaven is Zeus, who sees and governs all: leave thy bitter quarrel to him; forget not thy foes, but refrain from excess of wrath against them; for Time is god who makes rough ways smooth. Not heedless is the son of Agamemnon, who dwells by Crisa's pastoral shore; not heedless is the god who reigns by Acheron.

ELECTRA Nay, the best part of life hath passed away from me in hopelessness, and I have no strength left; I, who am pining away without children,- whom no loving champion shields,- but, like some despised alien, I serve in the halls of my father, clad in this mean garb, and standing at a meagre board.

CHORUS (strophe 3)

Piteous was the voice heard at his return, and piteous, as thy sire lay on the festal couch, when the straight, swift blow was dealt him with the blade of bronze. Guile was the plotter, Lust the slayer, dread parents of a dreadful shape; whether it was mortal that wrought therein, or god.

ELECTRA O that bitter day, bitter beyond all that have come to me; O that night, O the horrors of that unutterable feast, the ruthless deathstrokes that my father saw from the hands of twain, who took my life captive by treachery, who doomed me to woe! May the great god of Olympus give them sufferings in requital, and never may their splendour bring them joy, who have done such deeds!

CHORUS (antistrophe 3)

Be advised to say no more; canst thou not see what conduct it is which already plunges thee so cruelly in self-made miseries? Thou hast greatly aggravated thy troubles, ever breeding wars with thy sullen soul; but such strife should not be pushed to a conflict with the strong.

ELECTRA I have been forced to it,- forced by dread causes; I know my own passion, it escapes me not; but, seeing that the causes are so dire, will never curb these frenzied plaints, while life is in me. Who indeed, ye kindly sisterhood, who that thinks aright, would deem that any word of solace could avail me? Forbear, forbear, my comforters! Such ills must be numbered with those which have no cure; I can never know a respite from my sorrows, or a limit to this wailing.

CHORUS (epode)

At least it is in love, like a true-hearted mother, that I

dissuade thee from adding misery to miseries.

ELECTRA But what measure is there in my wretchedness? Say, how can it be right to neglect the dead? Was that impiety ever born in mortal? Never may I have praise of such; never when my lot is cast in pleasant places, may I cling to selfish ease, or dishonour my sire by restraining the wings of shrill lamentation!

For if the hapless dead is to lie in dust and nothingness, while the slayers pay not with blood for blood, all regard for man, all fear of heaven, will vanish from the earth.

LEADER OF THE CHORUS I came, my child, in zeal for thy welfare no less than for mine own; but if I speak not well, then be it as thou wilt; for we will follow thee.

ELECTRA I am ashamed, my friends, if ye deem me too impatient for my oft complaining; but, since a hard constraint forces me to this, bear with me. How indeed could any woman of noble nature refrain, who saw the calamities of a father's house, as I see them by day and night continually, not fading, but in the summer of their strength? I, who, first, from the mother that bore me have found bitter enmity; next, in mine own home I dwell with my father's murderers; they rule over me, and with them it rests to give or to withhold what I need.

And then think what manner of days I pass, when I see Aegisthus sitting on my father's throne, wearing the robes which he wore, and pouring libations at the hearth where he slew my sire; and when I see the outrage that crowns all, the murderer in our father's bed at our wretched mother's side, if mother she should be called, who is his wife; but so hardened is she that she lives with that accursed one, fearing no Erinys; nay, as if exulting in her deeds, having found the day on which she treacherously slew my father of old, she keeps it with dance and song, and month by month sacrifices sheep to the gods who have wrought her deliverance.

But I, hapless one, beholding it, weep and pine in the house, and bewail the unholy feast named after my sire,-

weep to myself alone; since I may not even indulge my grief to the full measure of my yearning. For this woman, in professions so noble, loudly upbraids me with such taunts as these: 'Impious and hateful girl, hast thou alone lost a father, and is there no other mourner in the world? An evil doom be thine, and may the gods infernal give thee no riddance from thy present laments.'

Thus she insults; save when any one brings her word that Orestes is coming: then, infuriated, she comes up to me, and cries;- 'Hast not thou brought this upon me? Is not this deed thine, who didst steal Orestes from my hands, and privily convey him forth? Yet be sure that thou shalt have thy due reward.' So she shrieks; and, aiding her, the renowned spouse at her side is vehement in the same strain,- that abject dastard, that utter pest, who fights his battles with the help of women. But I, looking ever for Orestes to come and end these woes, languish in my misery. Always intending to strike a blow, he has worn out every hope that I could conceive. In such a case, then, friends, there is no room for moderation or for reverence; in sooth, the stress of ills leaves no choice but to follow evil ways.

LEADER Say, is Aegisthus near while thou speakest thus, or absent from home?

ELECTRA Absent, certainly; do not think that I should have come to the doors, if he had been near; but just now he is afield.

LEADER Might I converse with thee more freely, if this is so?

ELECTRA He is not here, so put thy question; what wouldst thou?

LEADER I ask thee, then, what sayest thou of thy brother? Will he come soon, or is he delaying? I fain would know.

ELECTRA He promises to come; but he never fulfils the promise.

LEADER Yea, a man will pause on the verge of a great

work.

ELECTRA And yet I saved him without pausing.

LEADER Courage; he is too noble to fail his friends.

ELECTRA I believe it; or I should not have lived so long.

LEADER Say no more now; for I see thy sister coming from the house, Chrysothemis, daughter of the same sire and mother, with sepulchral gifts in her hands, such as are given to those in the world below. (CHRYSOTHEMIS enters from the palace. She is richly dressed.)

CHRYSOTHEMIS Why, sister, hast thou come forth once more to declaim thus at the public doors? Why wilt thou not learn with any lapse of time to desist from vain indulgence of idle wrath? Yet this I know,- that I myself am- grieved at our plight; indeed, could I find the strength, I would show what love I bear them. But now, in these troubled waters, 'tis best, methinks, to shorten sail; I care not to seem active, without the power to hurt. And would that thine own conduct were the same! Nevertheless, right is on the side of thy choice, not of that which I advise; but if I am to live in freedom, our rulers must be obeyed in all things.

ELECTRA Strange indeed, that thou, the daughter of such a sire as thine, shouldst forget him, and think only of thy mother! All thy admonitions to me have been taught by her; no word is thine own. Then take thy choice,- to be imprudent; or prudent, but forgetful of thy friends: thou, who hast just said that, couldst thou find the strength, thou wouldst show thy hatred of them; yet, when I am doing my utmost to avenge my sire, thou givest no aid, but seekest to turn thy sister from her deed.

Does not this crown our miseries with cowardice? For tell me,- Or let me tell thee,- what I should gain by ceasing from these laments? Do not live?- miserably, I know, yet well enough for me. And I vex them, thus rendering honour to the dead, if pleasure can be felt in that world. But thou, who tellest me of thy hatred, hatest in word alone, while in deeds thou art with the slayers of thy sire. I, then, would never yield to them, though I were promised the gifts which now make thee proud; thine be the richly-spread table and the life of luxury. For me, be it food enough that I do not wound mine own conscience; I covet not such privilege as thine,- nor wouldst thou, wert thou wise. But now, when thou mightest be called daughter of the noblest father among men, be called the child of thy mother; so shall thy baseness be most widely seen, in betrayal of thy dead sire and of thy kindred.

LEADER No angry word, I entreat! For both of you there is good in what is urged,- if thou, Electra, wouldst learn to profit by her counsel, and she, again, by thine.

CHRYSOTHEMIS For my part, friends, I am not wholly unused to her discourse; nor should I have touched upon this theme, had I not heard that she was threatened with a dread doom, which shall restrain her from her long-drawn laments.

ELECTRA Come, declare it then, this terror! If thou canst tell me of aught worse than my present lot, I will resist no more.

CHRYSOTHEMIS Indeed, I will tell thee all that I know. They purpose, if thou wilt not cease from these laments, to send thee where thou shalt never look upon the sunlight, but pass thy days in a dungeon beyond the borders of this land, there to chant thy dreary strain. Bethink thee, then, and do not blame me hereafter, when the blow hath fallen; now is the time to be wise.

ELECTRA Have they indeed resolved to treat me thus?

CHRYSOTHEMIS Assuredly, whenever Aegisthus comes home.

ELECTRA If that be all, then may he arrive with speed!

CHRYSOTHEMIS Misguided one! what dire prayer is this?

ELECTRA That he may come, if he hath any such intent.

CHRYSOTHEMIS That thou mayst suffer- what? Where are thy wits?

ELECTRA That I may fly as far as may be from you all.

CHRYSOTHEMIS But hast thou no care for thy present life?

ELECTRA Aye, my life is marvellously fair.

CHRYSOTHEMIS It might be, couldst thou only learn prudence.

ELECTRA Do not teach me to betray my friends.

CHRYSOTHEMIS I do not,- but to bend before the strong.

ELECTRA Thine be such flattery: those are not my ways.

CHRYSOTHEMIS Tis well, however, not to fall by folly.

ELECTRA I will fall, if need be, in the cause of my sire.

CHRYSOTHEMIS But our father, I know, pardons me for this.

ELECTRA It is for cowards to find peace in such maxims.

CHRYSOTHEMIS So thou wilt not hearken, and take my counsel?

ELECTRA No, verily; long may be it before I am so foolish.

CHRYSOTHEMIS Then I will go forth upon mine errand.

ELECTRA And whither goest thou? To whom bearest thou these offerings?

CHRYSOTHEMIS Our mother sends me with funeral libations for our sire.

ELECTRA How sayest thou? For her deadliest foe?

CHRYSOTHEMIS Slain by her own hand- so thou wouldest say.

ELECTRA What friend hath persuaded her? Whose wish was this?

CHRYSOTHEMIS The cause, I think, was some dread vision of the night.

ELECTRA Gods of our house! be ye with me- now at last!

CHRYSOTHEMIS Dost thou find any encouragement in this terror?

ELECTRA If thou wouldst tell me the vision, then I could answer.

CHRYSOTHEMIS Nay, I can tell but little of the story.

ELECTRA Tell what thou canst; a little word hath often marred, or made, men's fortunes.

CHRYSOTHEMIS 'Tis said that she beheld our sire, restored to the sunlight, at her side once more; then he took the sceptre,- Once his own, but now borne by Aegisthus,- and planted it at the hearth; and thence a fruitful bough sprang upward, wherewith the whole land of Mycenae was overshadowed. Such was the tale that I heard told by one who was present when she declared her dream to the Sun-god. More than this I know not,- save that she sent me by reason of that fear. So by the- gods of our house I beseech thee, hearken to me, and be not ruined by folly! For if thou repel me now, thou wilt come back to seek me in thy trouble.

ELECTRA Nay, dear sister, let none of these things in thy hands touch the tomb; for neither custom nor piety allows thee to dedicate gifts or bring libations to our sire from a hateful wife. No- to the winds with them or bury them deep in the earth, where none of them shall ever come near his place of rest; but, when she dies, let her find these treasures laid up for her below.

And were she not the most hardened of all women, she would never have sought to pour these offerings of enmity on the grave of him whom she slew. Think now if it is likely that the dead in the tomb should take these honours kindly at her hand, who ruthlessly slew him, like a foeman, and mangled him, and, for ablution, wiped off the blood-stains on his head? Canst thou believe that these things which thou bringest will absolve her of the murder?

It is not possible. No, cast these things aside; give him rather a lock cut from thine own tresses, and on my part, hapless that I am,-scant gifts these, but my best,- this hair, not glossy with unguents, and this girdle, decked with no rich ornament. Then fall down and pray that he himself may come in kindness from the world below, to aid us against our foes; and that the young Orestes may live to set his foot upon his foes in victorious might, that henceforth we may crown our father's tomb with wealthier hands than those which grace it now.

I think, indeed, I think that he also had some part in sending her these appalling dreams; still, sister, do this service, to help thyself, and me, and him, that most beloved of all men, who rests in the realm of Hades, thy sire and mine.

LEADER The maiden counsels piously; and thou, friend, wilt do her bidding, if- thou art wise.

CHRYSOTHEMIS I will. When a duty is clear, reason forbids that two voices should contend, and claims the hastening of the deed. Only, when I attempt this task, aid me with your silence, I entreat you, my friends; for, should my mother hear of it, methinks I shall yet have cause to rue my venture. (CHRYSOTHEMIS departs, to take the offerings to Agamemnon's grave.)

CHORUS (singing, strophe)

If I am not an erring seer and one who fails in wisdom,

justice, that hath sent the presage, will come, triumphant in her righteous strength,- will come ere long, my child, to avenge. There is courage in my heart, through those new tidings of the dream that breathes comfort. Not forgetful is thy sire, the lord of Hellas; not forgetful is the two-edged axe of bronze that struck the blow of old, and slew him with foul cruelty.

(antistrophe)

The Erinys of untiring feet, who is lurking in her dread ambush, will come, as with the march and with the might of a great host. For wicked ones have been fired with passion that hurried them to a forbidden bed, to accursed bridals, to a marriage stained with guilt of blood. Therefore am I sure that the portent will not fail to bring woe upon the partners in crime. Verily mortals cannot read the future in fearful dreams or oracles, if this vision of the night find not due fulfilment.

(epode)

O chariot-race of Pelops long ago, source of many a sorrow, what weary troubles hast thou brought upon this land! For since Myrtilus sank to rest beneath the waves, when a fatal and cruel hand hurled him to destruction out of the golden car, this house was never yet free from misery and violence. (CLYTEMNESTRA enters from the palace.)

CLYTEMNESTRA At large once more, it seems, thou rangest,- for Aegisthus is not here, who always kept thee at least from passing the gates, to shame thy friends. But now, since he is absent, thou takest no heed of me, though thou hast said of me oft-times, and to many, that I am a bold and lawless tyrant, who insults thee and thine. I am guilty of no insolence; I do but return the taunts that I often hear from thee.

Thy father- this is thy constant pretext- was slain by me. Yes, by me- I know it well; it admits of no denial; for justice slew him, and not I alone,- justice, whom it became thee to support, hadst thou been right-minded; seeing that this father of thine, whom thou art ever lamenting, was the one man of the Greeks who had the heart to sacrifice thy sister to the gods- he, the father, who had not shared the mother's pangs.

Come, tell me now, wherefore, or to please whom, did he sacrifice her? To please the Argives, thou wilt say? Nay, they had no right to slay my daughter. Or if, forsooth, it was to screen his brother Menelaus that he slew my child, was he not to pay me the penalty for that? Had not Menelaus two children, who should in fairness have been taken before my daughter, as sprung from the sire and mother who had caused that voyage? Or had Hades some strange desire to feast on my offspring, rather than on hers? Or had that accursed father lost all tenderness for the children of my womb, while he was tender to the children of Menelaus? Was not that the part of a callous and perverse parent? I think so, though differ from thy judgment; and so would say the dead, if she could speak. For myself, then, I view the past without dismay; but if thou deemest me perverse, see that thine own judgment is just, before thou blame thy neighbour.

ELECTRA This time thou canst not say that I have done anything to provoke such words from thee. But, if thou wilt give me leave, I fain would declare the truth, in the cause alike of my dead sire and of my sister.

CLYTEMNESTRA Indeed, thou hast my leave; and didst thou always address me in such a tone, thou wouldst be heard without pain.

ELECTRA Then I will speak. Thou sayest that thou hast slain my father. What word could bring thee deeper shame than that, whether the deed was just or not? But I must tell thee that thy deed was not just; no, thou wert drawn on to it by the wooing of the base man who is now thy spouse.

Ask the huntress Artemis what sin she punished when she stayed the frequent winds at Aulis; or I will tell thee; for we may not learn from her. My father- so I have heard- was once disporting himself in the grove of the goddess, when his footfall startled a dappled and antlered stag; he shot it, and chanced to utter a certain boast concerning its slaughter. Wroth thereat, the daughter of Leto detained the Greeks, that, in quittance for the wild creature's life, my father should yield up the life of his own child. Thus it befell that she was sacrificed; since the fleet had no other release, homeward or to Troy; and for that cause, under sore constraint and with sore reluctance, at last he slew her- not for the sake of Menelaus.

But grant- for I will take thine own plea- grant that the motive of his deed was to benefit his brother;- was that a reason for his dying by thy hand? Under what law? See that, in making such a law for men, thou make not trouble and remorse for thyself; for, if we are to take blood for blood, thou wouldst be the first to die, didst thou meet with thy desert.

But look if thy pretext is not false. For tell me, if thou wilt, wherefore thou art now doing the most shameless deeds of all,- dwelling as wife with that blood-guilty one, who first helped thee to slay my sire, and bearing children to him, while thou hast cast out the earlier-born, the stainless offspring of a stainless marriage. How can I praise these things? Or wilt thou say that this, too, is thy vengeance for thy daughter? Nay, shameful plea, if so thou plead; 'tis not well to wed an enemy for a daughter's sake.

But indeed I may not even counsel thee,- who shriekest that I revile my mother; and truly I think that to me thou art less a mother than mistress; so wretched is the life that I live, ever beset with miseries by thee and by thy partner. And that other, who scarce escaped thy hand, the hapless Orestes, is wearing out his ill-starred days in exile. Often hast thou charged me with rearing him to punish thy crime; and I would have done so, if I could, thou mayst be sure:-for that matter, denounce me to all, as disloyal, if thou wilt, or petulant, or impudent; for if I am accomplished in such ways, methinks I am no unworthy child of thee.

LEADER OF THE CHORUS I see that she breathes forth anger; but whether justice be with her, for this she seems to care no longer.

CLYTEMNESTRA (to the CHORUS) And what manner of care do I need to use against her, who hath thus insulted a mother, and this at her ripe age? Thinkest thou not that she would go forward to any deed, without shame?

ELECTRA Now be assured that I do feel shame for this, though thou believe it not; I know that my behaviour is unseemly, and becomes me ill. But then the enmity on thy part, and thy treatment, compel me in mine own despite to do thus; for base deeds are taught by base.

CLYTEMNESTRA Thou brazen one! Truly I and my sayings and my deeds give thee too much matter for words.

ELECTRA The words are thine, not mine; for thine is the action; and the acts find the utterance.

CLYTEMNESTRA Now by our lady Artemis, thou shalt not fail to pay for this boldness, so soon as Aegisthus returns.

ELECTRA Lo, thou art transported by anger, after granting me free speech, aid hast no patience to listen.

CLYTEMNESTRA Now wilt thou not hush thy clamour, or even suffer me to sacrifice, when I have permitted thee to speak unchecked?

ELECTRA I hinder not,- begin thy rites, I pray thee; and blame not my voice, for I shall say no more.

CLYTEMNESTRA Raise then, my handmaid, the offerings of many fruits, that I may uplift my prayers to this our king, for deliverance from my present fears. Lend now a gracious ear, O Phoebus our defender, to my words, though they be dark; for I speak not among friends, nor is it meet to unfold my whole thought to the light, while she stands near me, lest with her malice and her garrulous cry she spread some rash rumour throughout the town: but hear me thus, since on this wise I must speak.

That vision which I saw last night in doubtful dreams- if it hath come for my good, grant, Lycean king, that it be fulfilled; but if for harm, then let it recoil upon my foes. And if any are plotting to hurl me by treachery from the high estate which now is mine, permit them not; rather vouch. safe that, still living thus unscathed, I may bear sway over the house of the Atreidae and this realm, sharing prosperous days with the friends who share them now, and with those of my children from whom no enmity or bitterness pursues me.

O Lycean Apollo, graciously hear these prayers, and grant them to us all, even as we ask! For the rest, though I be silent, I deem that thou, a god, must know it; all things, surely, are seen by the sons of Zeus. (The PAEDAGOGUS enters.)

PAEDAGOGUS Ladies, might a stranger crave to know if this be the palace of the king Aegisthus?

LEADER It is, sir; thou thyself hast guessed aright.

PAEDAGOGUS And am I right in surmising that this lady is his consort? She is of queenly aspect.

LEADER Assuredly; thou art in the presence of the queen.

PAEDAGOGUS Hail, royal lady! I bring glad tidings to thee and to Aegisthus, from friend.

CLYTEMNESTRA I welcome the omen; but I would fain know from thee, first, who may have sent thee.

PAEDAGOGUS Phanoteus the Phocian, on a weighty mission.

CLYTEMNESTRA What is it, sir? Tell me: coming from a friend, thou wilt bring, I know; a kindly message.

PAEDAGOGUS Orestes is dead; that is the sum.

ELECTRA Oh, miserable that I am! I am lost this day!

CLYTEMNESTRA What sayest thou, friend, what sayest

thou?- listen not to her!

PAEDAGOGUS I said, and say again- Orestes is dead.

ELECTRA I am lost, hapless one, I am undone!

CLYTEMNESTRA (to ELECTRA) See thou to thine own concerns.- But do thou, sir, tell me exactly,-how did he perish?

PAEDAGOGUS I was sent for that purpose, and will tell thee all. Having gone to the renowned festival, the pride of Greece, for the Delphian games, when he heard the loud summons to the foot-race which was first to be decided, he entered the lists, a brilliant form, a wonder in the eyes of all there; and, having finished his course at the point where it began, he went out with the glorious meed of victory. To speak briefly, where there is much to tell, I know not the man whose deeds and triumphs have matched his; but one thing thou must know; in all the contests that the judges announced, he bore away the prize; and men deemed him happy, as oft as the herald proclaimed him an Argive, by name Orestes, son of Agamemnon, who once gathered the famous armament of Greece.

Thus far, 'twas well; but, when a god sends harm, not even the strong man can escape. For, on another day, when chariots were to try their speed at sunrise, he entered, with many charioteers. One was an Achaean, one from Sparta, two masters of yoked cars were Libyans; Orestes, driving Thessalian mares, came fifth among them; the sixth from Aetolia, with chestnut colts; a Magnesian was the seventh; the eighth, with white horses, was of Aenian stock; the ninth, from Athens, built of gods; there was a Boeotian too, making the tenth chariot.

They took their stations where the appointed umpires placed them by lot and ranged the cars; then, at the sound of the brazen trump, they started. All shouted to their horses, and shook the reins in their hands; the whole course was filled with the noise of rattling chariots; the dust flew upward; and all, in a confused throng, plied their goads unsparingly, each of them striving to pass the wheels and the snorting steeds of his rivals; for alike at their backs and at their rolling wheels the breath of the horses foamed and smote.

Orestes, driving close to the pillar at either end of the course, almost grazed it with his wheel each time, and, giving rein to the trace-horse on the right, checked the horse on the inner side. Hitherto, all the chariots had escaped overthrow; but presently the Aenian's hard-mouthed colts ran away, and, swerving, as they passed from the sixth into the seventh round, dashed their foreheads against the team of the Barcaean. Other mishaps followed the first, shock on shock and crash on crash, till the whole race-ground of Crisa was strewn with the wreck of the chariots.

Seeing this, the wary charioteer from Athens drew aside and paused, allowing the billow of chariots, surging in mid course, to go by. Orestes was driving last, keeping his horses behind,- for his trust was in the end; but when he saw that the Athenian was alone left in, he sent a shrill cry ringing through the ears of his swift colts, and gave chase. Team was brought level with team, and so they raced,-first one man, then the other. showing his head in front of the chariots.

Hitherto the ill-fated Orestes had passed safely through every round, steadfast in his steadfast car; at last, slackening his left rein while the horse was turning, unawares he struck the edge of the pillar; he broke the axle-box in twain; he was thrown over the chariot-rail; he was caught in the shapely reins; and, as he fell on the ground, his colts were scattered into the middle of the course.

But when the people saw him fallen from the car, a cry of pity went up for the youth, who had done such deeds and was meeting such a doom,- now dashed to earth, now tossed feet uppermost to the sky,- till the charioteers, with difficulty checking the career of his horses, loosed him, so covered with blood that no friend who saw it would have known the hapless corpse. Straightway they burned it on a pyre; and chosen men of Phocis are bringing in a small urn of bronze the sad dust of that mighty form, to find due burial in his fatherland.

Such is my story,- grievous to hear, if words can grieve; but for us, who beheld, the greatest of sorrows that these eyes have seen.

LEADER Alas, alas Now, methinks, the stock of our ancient masters hath utterly perished, root and branch.

CLYTEMNESTRA O Zeus, what shall I call these tidings,- glad tidings? Or dire, but gainful? 'Tis a bitter lot, when mine own calamities make the safety of my life.

PAEDAGOGUS Why art thou so downcast, lady, at this news?

CLYTEMNESTRA There is a strange power in motherhood; a mother may be wronged, but she never learns to hate her child.

PAEDAGOGUS Then it seems that we have come in vain.

CLYTEMNESTRA Nay, not in vain; how canst thou say 'in vain,' when thou hast brought an sure proofs of his death?- His, who sprang from mine own life, yet, forsaking me who had suckled and reared him, became an exile and an alien; and, after he went out of this land, he saw me no more; but, charging me with the murder of his sire, he uttered dread threats against me; so that neither by night nor by day could sweet sleep cover mine eyes, but from moment to moment I lived in fear of death. Now, however-since this day I am rid of terror from him, and from this girl,- that worse plague who shared my home, while still she drained my very life-blood,- now, methinks, for aught that she can threaten, I shall pass my days in peace.

ELECTRA Ah, woe is me! Now, indeed, Orestes, thy fortune may be lamented, when it is thus with thee, and thou art mocked by this thy mother! Is it not well?

CLYTEMNESTRA Not with thee; but his state is well.

ELECTRA Hear, Nemesis of him who hath lately died!

CLYTEMNESTRA She hath heard who should be heard, and hath ordained well.

ELECTRA Insult us, for this is the time of thy triumph.

CLYTEMNESTRA Then will not Orestes and thou silence me?

ELECTRA We are silenced; much less should we silence thee.

CLYTEMNESTRA Thy coming, sir, would deserve large recompense, if thou hast hushed her clamorous tongue.

PAEDAGOGUS Then I may take my leave, if all is well.

CLYTEMNESTRA Not so; thy welcome would then be unworthy of me, and of the ally who sent thee. Nay, come thou in; and leave her without, to make loud lament for herself and for her friends. (CLYTEMNESTRA and the PAEDAGOGUS enter the palace.)

ELECTRA How think ye? Was there not grief and anguish there, wondrous weeping and wailing of that miserable mother, for the son who perished by such a fate? Nay, she left us with a laugh! Ah, woe is me! Dearest Orestes, how is my life quenched by thy death! Thou hast torn away with the from my heart the only hopes which still were mine,- that thou wouldst live to return some day, an avenger of thy sire, and of me unhappy. But now- whither shall I turn? I am alone, bereft of thee, as of my father.

Henceforth I must be a slave again among those whom most I hate, my father's murderers. Is it not well with me? But never, at least, henceforward, will I enter the house to dwell with them; nay, at these gates I will lay me down, and here, without a friend, my days shall wither. Therefore, if any in the house be wroth, let them slay me; for 'tis a grace, if I die, but if I live, a pain; I desire life no more. (The following lines between ELECTRA and the CHORUS are chanted responsively.)

CHORUS (strophe 1)

Where are the thunderbolts of Zeus, or where is the bright Sun, if they look upon these things, and brand them not, but rest?

ELECTRA Woe, woe, ah me, ah me!

CHORUS O daughter, why weepest thou?

ELECTRA (with hands outstretched to heaven) Alas!

CHORUS Utter no rash cry!

ELECTRA Thou wilt break my heart!

CHORUS How meanest thou?

ELECTRA If thou suggest a hope concerning those who have surely passed to the realm below, thou wilt trample yet more upon my misery.

CHORUS (antistrophe 1)

Nay, I know how, ensnared by a woman for a chain of gold, the prince Amphiaraus found a grave; and now beneath the earth-

ELECTRA Ah me, ah me!

CHORUS -he reigns in fulness of force.

ELECTRA Alas!

CHORUS Alas indeed! for the murderess-

ELECTRA Was slain.

CHORUS Yea.

ELECTRA I know it, I know it; for a champion arose to avenge the mourning dead; but to me no champion remains; for he who yet was left hath been snatched away.

CHORUS (strophe 2)

Hapless art thou, and hapless is thy lot!

ELECTRA Well know I that, too well,- I, whose life is a torrent of woes dread and dark, a torrent that surges through all the months!

CHORUS We have seen the course of thy sorrow.

ELECTRA Cease, then, to divert me from it, when no more-

CHORUS How sayest thou?

ELECTRA -when no more can I have the comfort of hope from a brother, the seed of the same noble sire.

CHORUS (antistrophe 2)

For all men it is appointed to die.

ELECTRA What, to die as that ill-starred one died, amid the tramp of racing steeds, entangled in the reins that dragged him?

CHORUS Cruel was his doom, beyond thought!

ELECTRA Yea, surely; when in foreign soil, without ministry of my hands,-

CHORUS Alas!

ELECTRA -he is buried, ungraced by me with sepulture or with tears. (CHRYSOTHEMIS enters in excitement.)

CHRYSOTHEMIS Joy wings my feet, dear sister, not careful of seemliness, if I come with speed; for I bring joyful news, to relieve thy long sufferings and sorrows.

ELECTRA And whence couldst thou find help for my woes, whereof no cure can be imagined?

CHRYSOTHEMIS Orestes is with us,- know this from my lips, in living presence, as surely as thou seest me here.

ELECTRA What, art thou mad, poor girl? Art thou laughing at my sorrows, and thine own?

CHRYSOTHEMIS Nay, by our father's hearth, I speak

not in mockery; I tell thee that he is with us indeed.

ELECTRA Ah, woe is me! And from whom hast thou heard this tale, which thou believest so lightly?

CHRYSOTHEMIS I believe it on mine own knowledge, not on hearsay; I have seen clear proofs.

ELECTRA What hast thou seen, poor girl, to warrant thy belief? Whither, wonder hast thou turned thine eyes, that thou art fevered with this baneful fire?

CHRYSOTHEMIS Then, for the gods' love, listen, that thou mayest know my story, before deciding whether I am sane or foolish.

ELECTRA Speak on, then, if thou findest pleasure in speaking.

CHRYSOTHEMIS Well, thou shalt hear all that I have seen. When I came to our father's ancient tomb, I saw that streams of milk had lately flowed from the top of the mound, and that his sepulchre was encircled with garlands of all flowers that blow. I was astonished at the sight, and peered about, lest haply some one should be close to my side. But when I perceived that all the place was in stillness, I crept nearer to the tomb; and on the mound's edge I saw a lock of hair, freshly severed.

And the moment that I saw it, ah me, a familiar image rushed upon my soul, telling me that there I beheld a token of him whom most I love, Orestes. Then I took it in my hands, and uttered no ill-omened word, but the tears of joy straightway filled mine eyes. And I know well, as knew then, that this fair tribute has come from none but him. Whose part else was that, save mine and thine? And I did it not, I know,- nor thou; how shouldst thou?- when thou canst not leave this house, even to worship the gods, but at thy peril. Nor, again, does our mother's heart incline to do such deeds, nor could she have so done without our knowledge.

No, these offerings are from Orestes! Come, dear sister, courage! No mortal life is attended by a changeless fortune.

Ours was once gloomy; but this day, perchance, will seal the promise of much good.

ELECTRA Alas for thy folly! How I have been pitying thee!

CHRYSOTHEMIS What, are not my tidings welcome?

ELECTRA Thou knowest not whither or into what dreams thou wanderest.

CHRYSOTHEMIS Should I not know what mine own eyes have seen?

ELECTRA He is dead, poor girl; and thy hopes in that deliverer are gone: look not to him.

CHRYSOTHEMIS Woe, woe is me! From whom hast thou heard this?

ELECTRA From the man who was present when he perished.

CHRYSOTHEMIS And where is he? Wonder steals over my mind.

ELECTRA He is within, a guest not unpleasing to our mother.

CHRYSOTHEMIS Ah, woe is me! Whose, then, can have been those ample offerings to our father's tomb?

ELECTRA Most likely, I think, some one brought those gifts in memory of the dead Orestes.

CHRYSOTHEMIS Oh, hapless that I am! And I was bringing such news in joyous haste, ignorant, it seems, how dire was our plight; but now that I have come, I find fresh sorrows added to the old!

ELECTRA So stands thy case; yet, if thou wilt hearken to me, thou wilt lighten the load of our present trouble.

CHRYSOTHEMIS Can I ever raise the dead to life?

ELECTRA I meant not that; I am not so foolish.

CHRYSOTHEMIS What biddest thou, then, for which my strength avails?

ELECTRA That thou be brave in doing what I enjoin.

CHRYSOTHEMIS Nay, if any good can be done, I will not refuse,

ELECTRA Remember, nothing succeeds without toil.

CHRYSOTHEMIS I know it, and will share thy burden with all my power.

ELECTRA Hear, then, how I am resolved to act. As for the support of friends, thou thyself must know that we have none; Hades hath taken our friends away. and we two are left alone. I, so long as I heard that my brother still lived and prospered, had hopes that he would yet come to avenge the murder of our sire. But now that he is no more, I look next to thee, not to flinch from aiding me thy sister to slay our father's murderer, Aegisthus:- I must have no secret from thee more.

How long art thou to wait inactive? What hope is left standing, to which thine eyes can turn? Thou hast to complain that thou art robbed of thy father's heritage; thou hast to mourn that thus far thy life is fading without nuptial song or wedded love. Nay, and do not hope that such joys will ever be thine; Aegisthus is not so ill-advised as ever to permit that children should spring from thee or me for his own sure destruction. But if thou wilt follow my counsels, first thou wilt win praise of piety from our dead sire below, and from our brother too; next, thou shalt be called free henceforth, as thou wert born, and shalt find worthy bridals; for noble natures draw the gaze of all.

Then seest thou not what fair fame thou wilt win for thyself and for me, by hearkening to my word? What citizen or stranger, when he sees us, will not greet us with praises such as these?- 'Behold these two sisters, my friends, who saved their father's house; who, when their foes were firmly planted of yore, took their lives in their hands and stood forth as avengers of blood! Worthy of love are these twain, worthy of reverence from all; at festivals, and wherever the folk are assembled, let these be honoured of all men for their prowess.' Thus will every one speak of us, so that in life and in death our glory shall not fail.

Come, dear sister, hearken! Work with thy sire, share the burden of thy brother, win rest from woes for me and for thyself,- mindful of this, that an ignoble life brings shame upon the noble.

LEADER OF THE CHORUS In such case as this, forethought is helpful for those who speak and those who hear.

CHRYSOTHEMIS Yea, and before she spake, my friends, were she blest with a sound mind, she would have remembered caution, as she doth not remember it.

Now whither canst thou have turned thine eyes, that thou art arming thyself with such rashness, and calling me to aid thee? Seest thou not, thou art a woman, not a man, and no match for thine adversaries in strength? And their fortune prospers day by day, while ours is ebbing and coming to nought. Who, then, plotting to vanquish a foe so strong, shall escape without suffering deadly scathe? See that we change not our evil plight to worse, if any one hears these words. It brings us no relief or benefit, if, after winning fair fame, we die an ignominious death; for mere death is not the bitterest, but rather when one who wants to die cannot obtain even that boon.

Nay, I beseech thee, before we are utterly destroyed, and leave our house desolate, restrain thy rage! I will take care that thy words remain secret and harmless; and learn thou the prudence, at last though late, of yielding, when so helpless, to thy rulers.

LEADER Hearken; there is no better gain for mortals to win than foresight and a prudent mind.

ELECTRA Thou hast said nothing unlooked-for; I well

knew that thou wouldst reject what I proffered. Well! I must do this deed with mine own hand, and alone; for assuredly I will not leave it void.

CHRYSOTHEMIS Alas! Would thou hadst been so purposed on the day of our father's death! What mightst thou not have wrought?

ELECTRA My nature was the same then, but my mind less ripe.

CHRYSOTHEMIS Strive to keep such a mind through all thy life.

ELECTRA These counsels mean that thou wilt not share my deed.

CHRYSOTHEMIS No; for the venture is likely to bring disaster.

ELECTRA I admire thy prudence; thy cowardice I hate.

CHRYSOTHEMIS I will listen not less calmly when thou praise me.

ELECTRA Never fear to suffer that from me.

CHRYSOTHEMIS Time enough in the future to decide that.

ELECTRA Begone; there is no power to help in thee.

CHRYSOTHEMIS Not so; but in thee, no mind to learn.

ELECTRA Go, declare all this to thy mother!

CHRYSOTHEMIS But, again, I do not hate thee with such a hate.

ELECTRA Yet know at least to what dishonour thou bringest me.

CHRYSOTHEMIS Dishonour, no! I am only thinking of thy good.

ELECTRA Am I bound, then, to follow thy rule of right?

CHRYSOTHEMIS When thou art wise, then thou shalt be our guide.

ELECTRA Sad, that one who speaks so well should speak amiss!

CHRYSOTHEMIS Thou hast well described the fault to which thou cleavest.

ELECTRA How? Dost thou not think that I speak with justice?

CHRYSOTHEMIS But sometimes justice itself is fraught with harm.

ELECTRA I care not to live by such a law.

CHRYSOTHEMIS Well, if thou must do this, thou wilt praise me yet.

ELECTRA And do it I will, no whit dismayed by thee.

CHRYSOTHEMIS Is this so indeed? Wilt thou not change thy counsels?

ELECTRA No, for nothing is more hateful than bad counsel.

CHRYSOTHEMIS Thou seemest to agree with nothing that I urge.

ELECTRA My resolve is not new, but long since fixed.

CHRYSOTHEMIS Then I will go; thou canst not be brought to approve my words, nor to commend thy conduct.

ELECTRA Nay, go within; never will I follow thee, however much thou mayst desire it; it were great folly even to attempt an idle quest.

CHRYSOTHEMIS Nay, if thou art wise in thine own eyes, be such wisdom thine; by and by, when thou standest in evil plight, thou wilt praise my words. (CHRYSOTHEMIS goes into the palace.)

CHORUS (singing, strophe 1)

When we see the birds of the air, with sure instinct, careful to nourish those who give them life and nurture, why do not we pay these debts in like measure? Nay, by the lightning-flash of Zeus, by Themis throned in heaven, it is not long till sin brings sorrow.

Voice that comest to the dead beneath the earth, send a piteous cry, I pray thee, to the son of Atreus in that world, a joyless message of dishonour;

(antistrophe 1)

tell him that the fortunes of his house are now distempered; while, among his children, strife of sister with sister hath broken the harmony of loving days. Electra, forsaken, braves the storm alone; she bewails alway, hapless one, her father's fate, like the nightingale unwearied in lament; she recks not of death, but is ready to leave the sunlight, could she but quell the two Furies of her house. Who shall match such noble child of noble sire?

(strophe 2)

No generous soul deigns, by a base life, to cloud a fair repute, and leave a name inglorious; as thou, too, O my daughter, hast chosen to mourn all thy days with those that mourn, and hast spurned dishonour, that thou mightest win at once a twofold praise, as wise, and as the best of daughters.

(antistrophe 2)

May I yet see thy life raised in might and wealth above thy foes, even as now it is humbled beneath their hand! For I have found thee in no prosperous estate; and yet, for observance of nature's highest laws, winning the noblest renown, by thy piety towards Zeus. (ORESTES enters, with PYLADES and two attendants, one of them carrying a funeral urn.)

ORESTES Ladies, have we been directed aright, and are we on the right path to our goal?

LEADER OF THE CHORUS And what seekest thou? With what desire hast thou come?

ORESTES I have been searching for the home of Aegisthus.

LEADER Well, thou hast found it; and thy guide is blameless.

ORESTES Which of you, then, will tell those within that our company, long desired, hath arrived?

LEADER This maiden,- if the nearest should announce it.

ORESTES I pray thee, mistress, make it known in the house that certain men of Phocis seek Aegisthus.

ELECTRA Ah, woe is me! Surely ye are not bringing the visible proofs of that rumour which we heard?

ORESTES I know nothing of thy 'rumour'; but the aged Strophius charged me with tidings of Orestes.

ELECTRA What are they, sir? Ah, how I thrill with fear!

ORESTES He is dead; and in a small urn, as thou seest, we bring the scanty relics home.

ELECTRA Ah me unhappy! There, at last, before mine eyes, I see that woful burden in your hands

ORESTES If thy tears are for aught which Orestes hath suffered, know that yonder vessel holds his dust.

ELECTRA Ah, sir, allow me, then, I implore thee, if this urn indeed contains him, to take it in my hands,- that I may weep and wail, not for these ashes alone, but for myself and for all our house therewith!

ORESTES (to the attendants) Bring it and give it her, whoe'er she be; for she who begs this boon must be one who wished him no evil, but a friend, or haply a kinswoman in blood. (The urn is placed in ELECTRA'S hands.)

ELECTRA Ah, memorial of him whom I loved best on earth! Ah, Orestes, whose life hath no relic left save this,- how far from the hopes with which I sent thee forth is the manner in which I receive thee back! Now I carry thy poor dust in my hands; but thou wert radiant, my child, when I sped the forth from home! Would that I had yielded up my breath, ere, with these hands, I stole thee away, and sent thee to a strange land, and rescued the from death; that so thou mightest have been stricken down on that self-same day, and had thy portion in the tomb of thy sire!

But now, an exile from home and fatherland, thou hast perished miserably, far from thy sister; woe is me, these loving hands have not washed or decked thy corpse, nor taken up, as was meet, their sad burden from the flaming pyre. No! at the hands of strangers, hapless one, thou hast had those rites, and so art come to us, a little dust in a narrow urn.

Ah, woe is me for my nursing long ago, so vain, that I oft bestowed on thee with loving toil I For thou wast never thy mother's darling so much as mine; nor was any in the house thy nurse but I; and by thee I was ever called 'sister.' But now all this hath vanished in a day, with thy death; like a whirlwind, thou hast swept all away with thee. Our father is gone; I am dead in regard to thee; thou thyself hast perished: our foes exult; that mother, who is none, is mad with joy,- she of whom thou didst oft send me secret messages, thy heralds, saying that thou thyself wouldst appear as an avenger. But our evil fortune. thine and mine, hath reft all that away, and hath sent thee forth unto me thus,- no more the form that I loved so well, but ashes and an idle shade.

Ah me, ah me! O piteous dust! Alas, thou dear one, sent on a dire journey, how hast undone me,- undone me indeed, O brother mine!

Therefore take me to this thy home, me who am as nothing, to thy nothingness, that I may dwell with thee henceforth below; for when thou wert on earth, we shared alike; and now I fain would die, that I may not be parted from thee in the grave. For I see that the dead have rest from pain.

LEADER Bethink thee, Electra, thou art the child of mortal sire, and mortal was Orestes; therefore grieve not too much. This is a debt which all of us must pay.

ORESTES Alas, what shall I say? What words can serve me at this pass? I can restrain my lips no longer!

ELECTRA What hath troubled thee? Why didst thou say that?

ORESTES Is this the form of the illustrious Electra that I behold?

ELECTRA It is; and very grievous is her plight.

ORESTES Alas, then, for this miserable fortune!

ELECTRA Surely, sir, thy lament is not for me?

ORESTES O form cruelly, godlessly misused!

ELECTRA Those ill-omened words, sir, fit no one better than me.

ORESTES Alas for thy life, unwedded and all unblest!

ELECTRA Why this steadfast gaze, stranger, and these laments?

ORESTES How ignorant was I, then, of mine own sorrows!

ELECTRA By what that hath been said hast thou perceived this?

ORESTES By seeing thy sufferings, so many and so great.

ELECTRA And yet thou seest but a few of my woes.

ORESTES Could any be more painful to behold?

ELECTRA This, that I share the dwelling of the murderers.

ORESTES Whose murderers? Where lies the guilt at

which thou hintest?

ELECTRA My father's;- and then I am their slave perforce.

ORESTES Who is it that subjects thee to this constraint?

ELECTRA A mother-in name, but no mother in her deeds.

ORESTES How doth she oppress thee? With violence or with hardship?

ELECTRA With violence, and hardships, and all manner of ill.

ORESTES And is there none to succour, or to hinder?

ELECTRA None. I had one; and thou hast shown me his ashes.

ORESTES Hapless girl, how this sight hath stirred my pity!

ELECTRA Know, then, that thou art the first who ever pitied me.

ORESTES No other visitor hath ever shared thy pain.

ELECTRA Surely thou art not some unknown kinsman?

ORESTES I would answer, if these were friends who hear us.

ELECTRA Oh, they are friends; thou canst speak without mistrust.

ORESTES Give up this urn, then, and thou shalt be told all.

ELECTRA Nay, I beseech thee be not so cruel to me, sir!

ORESTES Do as I say, and never fear to do amiss.

ELECTRA I conjure thee, rob me not of my chief treasure!

ORESTES Thou must not keep it.

ELECTRA Ah woe is me for thee, Orestes, if I am not to give thee burial

ORESTES Hush!-no such word!-Thou hast no right to lament.

ELECTRA No right to lament for my dead brother?

ORESTES It is not meet for thee to speak of him thus.

ELECTRA Am I so dishonoured of the dead?

ORESTES Dishonoured of none:- but this is not thy part.

ELECTRA Yes, if these are the ashes of Orestes that I hold.

ORESTES They are not; a fiction dothed them with his name. (He gently takes the urn from her.)

ELECTRA And where is that unhappy one's tomb?

ORESTES There is none; the living have no tomb.

ELECTRA What sayest thou, boy?

ORESTES Nothing that is not true.

ELECTRA The man is alive?

ORESTES If there be life in me.

ELECTRA What? Art thou he?

ORESTES Look at this signet, once our father's, and judge if I speak truth.

ELECTRA O blissful day!

ORESTES Blissful, in very deed!

ELECTRA Is this thy voice?

ORESTES Let no other voice reply.

ELECTRA Do I hold thee in my arms?

ORESTES As mayest thou hold me always!

ELECTRA Ah, dear friends and fellow-citizens, behold Orestes here, who was feigned dead, and now, by that feigning hath come safely home!

LEADER We see him, daughter; and for this happy fortune a tear of joy trickles from our eyes. (The following lines between ORESTES and ELECTRA are chanted responsively.)

ELECTRA (strophe)

Offspring of him whom I loved best, thou hast come even now, thou hast come, and found and seen her whom thy heart desired!

ORESTES I am with thee;- but keep silence for a while.

ELECTRA What meanest thou?

ORESTES 'Tis better to be silent, lest some one within should hear.

ELECTRA Nay, by ever-virgin Artemis, I will never stoop to fear women, stay-at-homes, vain burdens of the ground!

ORESTES Yet remember that in women, too, dwells the spirit of battle; thou hast had good proof of that, I ween.

ELECTRA Alas! ah me! Thou hast reminded me of my sorrow, one which, from its nature, cannot be veiled, cannot be done away with, cannot forget!

ORESTES I know this also; but when occasion prompts, then will be the moment to recall those deeds.

ELECTRA (antistrophe)

Each moment of all time, as it comes, would be meet occasion for these my just complaints; scarcely now have I had my lips set free.

ORESTES I grant it; therefore guard thy freedom.

ELECTRA What must I do?

ORESTES When the season serves not, do not wish to speak too much.

ELECTRA Nay, who could fitly exchange speech for such silence, when thou hast appeared? For now I have seen thy face, beyond all thought and hope!

ORESTES Thou sawest it, when the gods moved me to come....

ELECTRA Thou hast told me of a grace above the first, if a god hath indeed brought thee to our house; I acknowledge therein the work of heaven.

ORESTES I am loth, indeed, to curb thy gladness, but yet this excess of joy moves my fear.

ELECTRA (epode)

O thou who, after many a year, hast deigned thus to gladden mine eyes by thy return, do not, now that thou hast seen me in all my woe-

ORESTES What is thy prayer?

ELECTRA -do not rob me of the comfort of thy face; do not force me to forego it!

ORESTES I should be wroth, indeed, if I saw another attempt it.

ELECTRA My prayer is granted?

ORESTES Canst thou doubt?

ELECTRA Ah, friends, I heard a voice that I could never have hoped to hear; nor could I have restrained my emotion in silence, and without cry, when I heard it.

Ah me! But now I have thee; thou art come to me with the

light of that dear countenance, which never, even in sorrow, could I forget. (The chant is concluded.)

ORESTES Spare all superfluous words; tell me not of our mother's wickedness, or how Aegisthus drains the wealth of our father's house by lavish luxury or aimless waste; for the story would not suffer thee to keep due limit. Tell me rather that which will serve our present need,- where we must show ourselves, or wait in ambush, that this our coming may confound the triumph of our foes.

And look that our mother read not thy secret in thy radiant face, when we twain have advanced into the house, but make lament, as for the feigned disaster; for when we have prospered, then there will be leisure to rejoice and exult in freedom.

ELECTRA Nay, brother, as it pleases thee, so shall be my conduct also; for all my joy is a gift from thee, and not mine own. Nor would I consent to win great good for myself at the cost of the least pain to thee; for so should I ill serve the divine power that befriends us now.

But thou knowest how matters stand here, I doubt not: thou must have beard that Aegisthus is from home, but our mother within;- and fear not that she will ever see my face lit up with smiles; for mine old hatred of her hath sunk into my heart; and, since I have beheld thee, for very joy I shall never cease to weep. How indeed should I cease, who have seen thee come home this day, first as dead, and then in life? Strangely hast thou wrought on me; so that, if my father should return alive, I should no longer doubt my senses, but should believe that I saw him. Now, therefore, that thou hast come to me so wondrously, command me as thou wilt; for, had I been alone, I should have achieved one of two things,- a noble deliverance, or a noble death.

ORESTES Thou hadst best be silent; for I hear some one within preparing to go forth.

ELECTRA (to ORESTES AND PYLADES) Enter, sirs; especially as ye bring that which no one could repulse from

these doors, though he receive it without joy. (The PAEDA-
GOGUS enters from the palace.)

PAEDAGOGUS Foolish and senseless children! Are ye
weary of your lives, or was there no wit born in you, that ye
see not how ye stand, not on the brink, but in the very midst
of deadly perils? Nay, had I not kept watch this long while at
these doors, your plans would have been in the house before
yourselves; but, as it is, my care shielded you from that. Now
have done with this long discourse, these insatiate cries of
joy, and pass within; for in such deeds delay is evil, and 'tis
well to make an end.

ORESTES What, then, will be my prospects when I enter?

PAEDAGOGUS Good; for thou art secured from recogni-
tion.

ORESTES Thou hast reported me, I presume, as dead?

PAEDAGOGUS Know that here thou art numbered with
the shades.

ORESTES Do they rejoice, then, at these tidings? Or
what say they?

PAEDAGOGUS I will tell thee at the end; meanwhile, all
is well for us on their party-even that which is not well.

ELECTRA Who is this, brother? I pray thee, tell me.

ORESTES Dost thou not perceive?

ELECTRA I cannot guess.

ORESTES Knowest thou not the man to whose hands
thou gavest me once?

ELECTRA What man? How sayest thou?

ORESTES By whose hands, through thy forethought, I
was secretly conveyed forth to Phocian soil.

ELECTRA Is this he in whom, alone of many, I found a

true ally of old, when our sire was slain?

ORESTES 'Tis he; question me no further.

ELECTRA O joyous day! O sole preserver of Agamemnon's house, how hast thou come? Art thou he indeed, who didst save my brother and myself from many sorrows? O dearest hands; O messenger whose feet were kindly servants! How couldst thou be with me so long, and remain unknown, nor give a ray of light, but afflict me by fables, while possessed of truths most sweet? Hail, father,- for 'tis a father that I seem to behold! All hail,- and know that I have hated thee, and loved thee, in one day, as never man before!

PAEDAGOGUS Enough, methinks; as for the story of the past, many are the circling nights, and days as many, which shall show it thee, Electra, in its fulness. (To ORESTES and PYLADES) But this is my counsel to you twain, who stand there- now is the time to act; now Clytemnestra is alone,- no man is now within: but, if ye pause, consider that ye will have to fight, not with the inmates alone, but with other foes more numerous and better skilled.

ORESTES Pylades, this our task seems no longer to crave many words, but rather that we should enter the house forthwith,- first adoring the shrines of my father's gods, who keep these gates. (ORESTES and PYLADES enter the Palace, followed by the PAEDAGOGUS.- ELECTRA remains outside.)

ELECTRA O King Apollo! graciously hear them, and hear me besides, who so oft have come before thine altar with such gifts as my devout hand could bring! And now, O Lycean Apollo, with such vows as I can make, I pray thee, I supplicate, I implore, grant us thy benignant aid in these designs, and show men how impiety is rewarded by the gods! (ELECTRA enters the palace.)

CHORUS (singing) Behold how Ares moves onward, breathing deadly vengeance, against which none may strive!

Even now the pursuers of dark guilt have passed beneath

yon roof, the hounds which none may flee. Therefore the vision of my soul shall not long tarry in suspense.

The champion of the spirits infernal is ushered with stealthy feet into the house, the ancestral palace of his sire, bearing keen-edged death in his hands; and Hermes, son of Maia, who hath shrouded the guile in darkness, leads him forward, even to the end, and delays no more. (ELECTRA enters from the palace.)

ELECTRA (strophe)

Ah, dearest friends, in a moment the men will do the deed;- but wait in silence.

CHORUS How is it?- what do they now?

ELECTRA She is decking the urn for burial, and those two stand close to her

CHORUS And why hast thou sped forth?

ELECTRA To guard against Aegisthus entering before we are aware.

CLYTEMNESTRA (within) Alas! Woe for the house forsaken of friends and filled with murderers!

ELECTRA A cry goes up within:- hear ye not, friends?

CHORUS I heard, ah me, sounds dire to hear, and shuddered!

CLYTEMNESTRA (within) O hapless that I am!- Aegisthus, where, where art thou?

ELECTRA Hark, once more a voice resounds I

CLYTEMNESTRA (within) My son, my son, have pity on thy mother!

ELECTRA Thou hadst none for him, nor for the father that begat him.

CHORUS Ill-fated realm and race, now the fate that hath

pursued thee day by day is dying,- is dying!

CLYTEMNESTRA (within) Oh, I am smitten!

ELECTRA Smite, if thou canst, once more!

CLYTEMNESTRA (within) Ah, woe is me again!

ELECTRA Would that the woe were for Aegisthus too!

CHORUS The curses are at work; the buried live; blood flows for blood, drained from the slayers by those who died of yore. (ORESTES and PYLADES enter from the palace., antistrophe)

Behold, they come! That red hand reeks with sacrifice to Ares; nor can I blame the deed.

ELECTRA Orestes, how fare ye?

ORESTES All is well within the house, if Apollo's oracle spake well.

ELECTRA The guilty one is dead?

ORESTES Fear no more that thy proud mother will ever put thee to dishonour.

CHORUS Cease; for I see Aegisthus full in view.

ELECTRA Rash boys, back, back!

ORESTES Where see ye the man?

ELECTRA Yonder, at our mercy, be advances from the suburb, full of joy.

CHORUS Make with all speed for the vestibule; that, as your first task prospered. so this again may prosper now.

ORESTES Fear not,- we will perform it.

ELECTRA Haste, then, whither thou wouldst.

ORESTES See, I am gone.

ELECTRA I will look to matters here. (ORESTES and

PYLADES go back into the palace.)

CHORUS 'Twere well to soothe his ear with some few words of seeming gentleness, that he may rush blindly upon the struggle with his doom. (AEGISTHUS enters.)

AEGISTHUS Which of you can tell me, where are those Phocian strangers, who, 'tis said, have brought us tidings of Orestes slain in the wreck of his chariot? Thee, thee I ask, yes, thee, in former days so bold,- for methinks it touches thee most nearly; thou best must know, and best canst tell.

ELECTRA I know assuredly; else were I a stranger to the fortune of my nearest kinsfolk.

AEGISTHUS Where then may be the strangers? Tell me.

ELECTRA Within; they have found a way to the heart of their hostess.

AEGISTHUS Have they in truth reported him dead?

ELECTRA Nay, not reported only; they have shown him.

AEGISTHUS Can I, then, see the corpse with mine own eyes?

ELECTRA Thou canst, indeed; and 'tis no enviable sight.

AEGISTHUS Indeed, thou hast given me a joyful greeting, beyond thy wont.

ELECTRA Joy be thine, if in these things thou findest joy.

AEGISTHUS Silence, I say, and throw wide the gates, for all Mycenaeans and Argives to behold; that, if any of them were once buoyed on empty hopes from this man, now, seeing him dead, they may receive my curb, instead of waiting till my chastisement make them wise perforce!

ELECTRA No loyalty is lacking on my part; time hath

taught me the prudence of concord with the stronger. (The central doors of the palace are thrown open and a shrouded corpse is disclosed. ORESTES and PYLADES stand near it.)

AEGISTHUS O Zeus, I behold that which hath not fallen save by the doom of jealous Heaven; but, if Nemesis attend that word, be it unsaid!

Take all the covering from the face, that kinship, at least, may receive the tribute of lament from me also.

ORESTES Lift the veil thyself; not my part this, but thine, to look upon these relics, and to greet them kindly.

AEGISTHUS 'Tis good counsel, and I will follow it.- (To ELECTRA) But thou-call me Clytemnestra, if she is within.

ORESTES Lo, she is near thee: turn not thine eyes elsewhere. (AEGISTHUS removes the face-cloth from the corpse.)

AEGISTHUS O, what sight is this!

ORESTES Why so scared? Is the face so strange?

AEGISTHUS Who are the men into whose mid toils I have fallen, hapless that I am?

ORESTES Nay, hast thou not discovered ere now that the dead, as thou miscallest them, are living?

AEGISTHUS Alas, I read the riddle: this can be none but Orestes who speaks to me!

ORESTES And, though so good a prophet, thou wast deceived so long?

AEGISTHUS Oh lost, undone! Yet suffer me to say one word...

ELECTRA In heaven's name, my brother, suffer him not to speak further, or to plead at length! When mortals are in the meshes of fate, how can such respite avail one who is to die? No,- slay him forthwith, and cast his corpse to the creatures from whom such as he should have burial, far from our sight! To me, nothing but this can make amends for the woes of the past.

ORESTES (to AEGISTHUS) Go in, and quickly; the issue here is not of words, but of thy life.

AEGISTHUS Why take me into the house? If this deed be fair, what need of darkness? Why is thy hand not prompt to strike?

ORESTES Dictate not, but go where thou didst slay my father, that in the same place thou mayest die.

AEGISTHUS Is this dwelling doomed to see all woes of Pelops' line, now, and in time to come?

ORESTES Thine, at least; trust my prophetic skill so far.

AEGISTHUS The skill thou vauntest belonged not to thy sire.

ORESTES Thou bandiest words, and our going is delayed. Move forward!

AEGISTHUS Lead thou.

ORESTES Thou must go first.

AEGISTHUS Lest I escape thee?

ORESTES No, but that thou mayest not choose how to die; I must not spare thee any bitterness of death. And well it were if this judgment came straight-way upon all who dealt in lawless deeds, even the judgment of the sword: so should not wickedness abound. (ORESTES and PYLADES drive AEGISTHUS into the palace.)

CHORUS (singing) O house of Atreus, through how many sufferings hast thou come forth at last in freedom, crowned with good by this day's enterprise!

THE END

Philoctetes

Dramatis Personae

ULYSSES, King of Ithaca
NEOPTOLEMUS, son of Achilles
PHILOCTETES, son of Poeas and Companion of HERCULES
A SPY
HERCULES
CHORUS, composed of the companions of ULYSSES and
NEOPTOLEMUS

A lonely region on the shore of Lemnos, before a steep cliff in which is the entrance to PHILOCTETES' cave. ULYSSES, NEOPTOLEMUS and an attendant enter.

ULYSSES At length, my noble friend, thou bravest son Of a brave father- father of us all, The great Achilles- we have reached the shore Of sea-girt Lemnos, desert and forlorn, Where never tread of human step is seen, Or voice of mortal heard, save his alone, Poor Philoctetes, Poeas' wretched son, Whom here I left; for such were my commands From Grecia's chiefs, when by his fatal wound Oppressed, his groans and execrations dreadful Alarmed our hosts, our sacred rites profaned, And interrupted holy sacrifice. But why should I repeat the tale? The time Admits not of delay. We must not linger, Lest he discover our arrival here, And all our purposed fraud to draw him hence Be ineffectual. Lend me then thy aid. Surveying round thee, canst thou see a rock With double entrance- to the sun's warm rays In winter open, and in summer's heat Giving free passage to the welcome breeze? A little to the left there is a fountain Of living water, where, if yet he breathes, He slakes his thirst. If aught thou seest of this Inform me; so shall each to each impart Counsel most fit, and serve our common cause.

NEOPTOLEMUS (leaving ULYSSES a little behind him) If I mistake not, I behold a cave, E'en such as thou describst.

ULYSSES Dost thou? which way?

NEOPTOLEMUS Yonder it is; but no path leading thither, Or trace of human footstep.

ULYSSES In his cell A chance but he hath lain down to rest: Look if he hath not.

NEOPTOLEMUS (advancing to the cave) Not a creature there.

ULYSSES Nor food, nor mark of household preparation?

NEOPTOLEMUS A rustic bed of scattered leaves.

ULYSSES What more?

NEOPTOLEMUS A wooden bowl, the work of some rude hand, With a few sticks for fuel.

ULYSSES This is all His little treasure here.

NEOPTOLEMUS Unhappy man! Some linen for his wounds.

ULYSSES This must be then His place of habitation; far from hence He cannot roam; distempered as he is, It were impossible. He is but gone A little way for needful food, or herb Of power to 'suage and mitigate his pain, Wherefore despatch this servant to some place Of observation, whence he may espy His every motion, lest he rush upon us. There's not a Grecian whom his soul so much Could wish to crush beneath him as Ulysses. (He makes a signal to the Attendant. who retires.)

NEOPTOLEMUS He's gone to guard each avenue; and

now, If thou hast aught of moment to impart Touching our
purpose, say it; I attend.

ULYSSES Son of Achilles, mark me well! Remember,
What we are doing not on strength alone, Or courage, but
oil conduct will depend; Therefore if aught uncommon be
proposed, Strange to thy ears and adverse to thy nature,
Reflect that 'tis thy duty to comply, And act conjunctive with
me.

NEOPTOLEMUS Well, what is it?

ULYSSES We must deceive this Philoctetes; that Will
be thy task. When he shall ask thee who And what thou art,
Achilles'son reply- Thus far within the verge of truth, no
more. Add that resentment fired thee to forsake The Grecian fleet, and seek thy native soil, Unkindly used by those
who long with vows Had sought thy aid to humble haughty
Troy, And when thou cam'st, ungrateful as they were. The
arms of great Achilles, thy just right, Gave to Ulysses. Here
thy bitter taunts And sharp invectives liberally bestow On
me. Say what thou wilt, I shall forgive, And Greece will not
forgive thee if thou dost not; For against Troy thy efforts are
all vain Without his arrows. Safely thou mayst hold Friendship and converse with him, but I cannot. Thou wert not
with us when the war began, Nor bound by solemn oath to
join our host, As I was; me he knows, and if he find That I
am with thee, we are both undone. They must be ours then,
these all-conquering arms; Remember that. I know thy noble nature Abhors the thought of treachery or fraud. But
what a glorious prize is victory! Therefore be bold; we will
be just hereafter. Give to deceit and me a little portion Of
one short day, and for thy future life Be called the holiest,
worthiest, best of men.

NEOPTOLEMUS What but to hear alarms my conscious
soul, Son of Laertes, I shall never practise. I was not born
to flatter or betray; Nor I, nor he- the voice of fame reports-
Who gave me birth. What open arms can do Behold me
prompt to act, but ne'er to fraud Will I descend. Sure we can
more than match In strength a foe thus lame and impotent.

I came to be a helpmate to thee, not A base betrayer; and, O king! believe me, Rather, much rather would I fall by virtue Than rise by guilt to certain victory.

ULYSSES O noble youth! and worthy of thy sire! When I like thee was young, like thee of strength And courage boastful, little did I deem Of human policy; but long experience Hath taught me, son, 'tis not the powerful arm, But soft enchanting tongue that governs all.

NEOPTOLEMUS And thou wouldst have me tell an odious falsehood?

ULYSSES He must be gained by fraud.

NEOPTOLEMUS By fraud? And why Not by persuasion?

ULYSSES He'll not listen to it; And force were vainer still.

NEOPTOLEMUS What mighty power Hath he to boast?

ULYSSES His arrows winged with death Inevitable.

NEOPTOLEMUS Then it were not safe E'en to approach him.

ULYSSES No; unless by fraud He be secured.

NEOPTOLEMUS And thinkst thou 'tis not base To tell a lie then?

ULYSSES Not if on that lie Depends our safety.

NEOPTOLEMUS Who shall dare to tell it Without a blush?

ULYSSES We need not blush at aught That may promote our interest and success.

NEOPTOLEMUS But where's the interest that should bias me?

Come he or not to Troy, imports it aught To Neoptolemus?

ULYSSES Troy cannot fall Without his arrows.

NEOPTOLEMUS Saidst thou not that I Was destined to
destroy her?

ULYSSES Without them Naught canst thou do, and they
without thee nothing.

NEOPTOLEMUS Then I must have them.

ULYSSES When thou hast, remember A double prize
awaits thee.

NEOPTOLEMUS What, Ulysses?

ULYSSES The glorious names of valiant and of wise.

NEOPTOLEMUS Away! I'll do it. Thoughts of guilt or
shame

No more appal me.

ULYSSES Wilt thou do it then? Wilt thou remember
what I told thee of?

NEOPTOLEMUS Depend on 't; I have promised- that's
sufficient.

ULYSSES Here then remain thou; I must not be seen.
If thou stay long, I'll send a faithful spy, Who in a sailor's
habit well disguised May pass unknown; of him, from time
to time, What best may suit our purpose thou shalt know.
I'll to the ship. Farewell! and may the god Who brought us
here, the fraudful Mercury, And great Minerva, guardian
of our country, And ever kind to me, protect us still! (UL-
YSSES goes out as the CHORUS enters. The following lines
are chanted responsively between NEOPTOLEMUS and the
CHORUS.)

CHORUS (strophe 1)

Master, instruct us, strangers as we are, What we may

utter, what we must conceal. Doubtless the man we seek will entertain Suspicion of us; how are we to act? To those alone belongs the art to rule Who bear the sceptre from the hand of Jove; To thee of right devolves the power supreme, From thy great ancestors delivered down; Speak then, our royal lord, and we obey.

NEOPTOLEMUS (systema 1)

If you would penetrate yon deep recess To seek the cave where Philoctetes lies, Go forward; but remember to return When the poor wanderer comes this way, prepared To aid our purpose here if need require.

CHORUS (antistrophe 1)

O king! we ever meant to fix our eyes On thee, and wait attentive to thy will; But, tell us, in what part is he concealed? 'Tis fit we know the place, lest unobserved He rush upon us. Which way doth it lie? Seest thou his footsteps leading from the cave, Or hither bent?

NEOPTOLEMUS (advancing towards the cave, systema 2)

Behold the double door Of his poor dwelling, and the flinty bed.

CHORUS And whither is its wretched master gone?

NEOPTOLEMUS Doubtless in search of food, and not far off,

For such his manner is; accustomed here, So fame reports, to pierce with winged arrows His savage prey for daily sustenance, His wound still painful, and no hope of cure.

CHORUS (strophe 2)

Alas! I pity him. Without a friend, Without a fellow-sufferer, left alone, Deprived of all the mutual joys that flow From sweet society- distempered too! How can he bear it? O unhappy race Of mortal man! doomed to an endless round Of sorrows, and immeasurable woe!

(antistrophe 2)

Second to none in fair nobility Was Philoctetes, of illustrious race; Yet here he lies, from every human aid Far off removed, in dreadful solitude, And mingles with the wild and savage herd; With them in famine and in misery Consumes his days, and weeps their common fate, Unheeded, save when babbling echo mourns In bitterest notes responsive to his woe.

NEOPTOLEMUS (systema 3)

And yet I wonder not; for if aright I judge, from angry heaven the sentence came, And Chrysa was the cruel source of all; Nor doth this sad disease inflict him still Incurable, without assenting gods? For so they have decreed, lest Troy should fall Beneath his arrows ere the' appointed time Of its destruction come.

CHORUS (strophe 3)

No more, my son!

NEOPTOLEMUS What sayst thou?

CHORUS Sure I heard a dismal groan Of some afflicted wretch.

NEOPTOLEMUS Which way?

CHORUS E'en now I hear it, and the sound as of some step Slow-moving this way. He is not far from us. His plaints are louder now.

(antistrophe 3)

Prepare, my son!

NEOPTOLEMUS For what?

CHORUS New troubles; for behold he comes! Not like the shepherd with his rural pipe And cheerful song, but groaning heavily. Either his wounded foot against some thorn Hath struck, and pains him sorely, or perchance He hath espied from far some ship attempting To enter this inhospitable port, And hence his cries to save it from destruction. (PHI-LOCTETES enters, clad in rags. He moves with difficulty and is obviously suffering pain from his injured foot.)

PHILOCTETES Say, welcome strangers, what disastrous fate

Led you to this inhospitable shore, Nor haven safe, nor habitation fit Affording ever? Of what clime, what race? Who are ye? Speak! If I may trust that garb, Familiar once to me, ye are of Greece, My much-loved country. Let me hear the sound Of your long wished-for voices. Do not look With horror on me, but in kind compassion Pity a wretch deserted and forlorn In this sad place. Oh! if ye come as friends, Speak then, and answer- hold some converse with me, For this at least from man to man is due.

NEOPTOLEMUS Know, stranger, first what most thou seemst to wish;

We are of Greece.

PHILOCTETES Oh! happiness to hear! After so many years of dreadful silence, How welcome was that sound! Oh! tell me, son, What chance, what purpose, who conducted thee? What brought thee thither, what propitious gale? Who art thou? Tell me all- inform me quickly.

NEOPTOLEMUS Native of Scyros, hither I return; My name is Neoptolemus, the son Of brave Achilles. I have told thee all.

PHILOCTETES Dear is thy country, and thy father dear To me, thou darling of old Lycomede; But tell me in what fleet, and whence thou cam'st.

NEOPTOLEMUS From Troy.

PHILOCTETES From Troy? I think thou wert not with us When first our fleet sailed forth.

NEOPTOLEMUS Wert thou then there? Or knowst thou aught of that great enterprise?

PHILOCTETES Know you not then the man whom you behold?

NEOPTOLEMUS How should I know whom I had never seen?

PHILOCTETES Have you ne'er heard of me, nor of my name?

Hath my sad story never reached your ear?

NEOPTOLEMUS Never.

PHILOCTETES Alas! how hateful to the gods, How very poor a wretch must I be then, That Greece should never hear of woes like mine! But they who sent me hither, they concealed them, And smile triumphant, whilst my cruel wounds Grow deeper still. O, sprung from great Achilles! Behold before thee Poeas' wretched son, With whom, a chance but thou hast heard, remain The dreadful arrows of renowned Alcides, E'en the unhappy Philoctetes- him Whom the Atreidae and the vile Ulysses Inhuman left, distempered as I was By the envenomed serpent's deep-felt wound. Soon as they saw that, with long toil oppressed, Sleep had o'ertaken me on the hollow rock, There did they leave me when from Chrysa's shore They bent their fatal course; a little food And these few rags were all they would bestow. Such one day be their fate! Alas! my son, How dreadful, thinkst thou, was that waking to me, When from my sleep I rose and saw them not! How did I weep! and mourn my wretched state! When not a ship remained of all the fleet That brought me here- no kind companion left To minister or needful food or balm To my sad wounds. On every side I looked, And nothing saw but woe; of that indeed Measure too full. For day succeeded day, And still no comfort came; myself alone Could to myself the means of life afford, In this poor grotto. On my bow I lived: The winged dove, which my sharp arrow slew, With pain I brought into my little hut, And feasted there; then from the broken ice I slaked my thirst, or crept into the wood For useful fuel; from the stricken flint I drew the latent spark, that warms me still And still revives. This with my humble roof

Preserve me, son. But, oh! my wounds remain. Thou seest an island desolate and waste; No friendly port nor hopes of gain to tempt, Nor host to welcome in the traveller; Few seek the wild inhospitable shore. By adverse winds, sometimes th' unwilling guests, As well thou mayst suppose, were hither driven; But when they came, they only pitied me, Gave me a little food, or better garb To shield me from the cold; in vain I prayed That they would bear me to my native soil, For none would listen. Here for ten long years Have I remained, whilst misery and famine Keep fresh my wounds, and double my misfortune. This have th' Atreidae and Ulysses done, And may the gods with equal woes repay them!

LEADER OF THE CHORUS O, son of Poeas! well might those, who came

And saw thee thus, in kind compassion weep; I too must pity thee- I can no more.

NEOPTOLEMUS I can bear witness to thee, for I know By sad experience what th' Atreidae are, And what Ulysses.

PHILOCTETES Hast thou suffered then? And dost thou hate them too?

NEOPTOLEMUS Oh! that these hands Could vindicate my wrongs! Mycenae then And Sparta should confess that Scyros boasts Of sons as brave and valiant as their own.

PHILOCTETES O noble youth! But wherefore cam'st thou hither?

Whence this resentment?

NEOPTOLEMUS I will tell thee all, If I can bear to tell it. Know then, soon As great Achilles died-

PHILOCTETES Oh, stay, my son! Is then Achilles dead?

NEOPTOLEMUS He is, and not By mortal hand, but by Apollo's shaft Fell glorious.

PHILOCTETES Oh! most worthy of each other, The slayer and the slain! Permit me, son, To mourn his fate, ere I attend to thine.

NEOPTOLEMUS Alas! thou needst not weep for others' woes,

Thou hast enough already of thy own.

PHILOCTETES 'Tis very true; and therefore to thy tale.

NEOPTOLEMUS Thus then it was. Soon as Achilles died, Phoenix, the guardian of his tender years, Instant sailed forth, and sought me out at Scyros; With him the wary chief Ulysses came. They told me then (or true or false I know not), My father dead, by me, and me alone Proud Troy must fall. I yielded to their prayers; I hoped to see at least the dear remains Of him whom living I had long in vain Wished to behold. Safe at Sigeum's port Soon we arrived. In crowds the numerous host Thronged to embrace me, called the gods to witness In me once more they saw their loved Achilles To life restored; but he, alas! was gone. I shed the duteous tear, then sought my friends Th' Atreidae friends I thought 'em!- claimed the arms Of my dead father, and what else remained His late possession: when- O cruel words! And wretched I to hear them- thus they answered: "Son of Achilles, thou in vain demandst Those arms already to Ulysses given; The rest be thine." I wept. "And is it thus," Indignant I replied, "ye dare to give My right away?" "Know, boy," Ulysses cried, "That right was mine. and therefore they bestowed The boon on me: me who preserved the arms, And him who bore them too." With anger fired At this proud speech, I threatened all that rage Could dictate to me if he not returned them. Stung with my words, yet calm, he answered me: "Thou wert not with us; thou wert in a place Where thou shouldst not have been; and since thou meanst

To brave us thus, know, thou shalt never bear Those arms with thee to Scyros; 'tis resolved." Thus injured, thus deprived of all I held Most precious, by the worst of men, I left The hateful place, and seek my native soil. Nor do

I blame so much the proud Ulysses As his base masters-
army, city, all Depend on those who rule. When men grow
vile The guilt is theirs who taught them to be wicked. I've
told thee all, and him who hates the Atreidae I hold a friend
to me and to the gods.

CHORUS (singing) O Earth! thou mother of great Jove,
Embracing all with universal love, Author benign of every
good, Through whom Pactolus rolls his golden flood! To thee,
whom in thy rapid car Fierce lions draw, I rose and made
my prayer- To thee I made my sorrows known, When from
Achilles' injured son Th' Atreidae gave the prize, that fatal
day When proud Ulysses bore his arms away.

PHILOCTETES I wonder not, my friend, to see you here,
And I believe the tale; for well I know The man who wronged
you, know the base Ulysses Falsehood and fraud dwell on
his lips, and nought That's just or good can be expected from
him. But strange it is to me that, Ajax present, He dare attempt it.

NEOPTOLEMUS Ajax is no more; Had he been living, I
had ne'er been spoiled Thus of my right.

PHILOCTETES Is he then dead?

NEOPTOLEMUS He is.

PHILOCTETES Alas! the son of Tydeus, and that slave,
Sold by his father Sisyphus, they live, Unworthy as they
are.

NEOPTOLEMUS Alas! they do, And flourish still.

PHILOCTETES My old and worthy friend The Pylian
sage, how is he? He could see Their arts, and would have
given them better counsels.

NEOPTOLEMUS Weighed down with grief he lives, but
most unhappy,

Weeps his lost son, his dear Antilochus.

PHILOCTETES O double woe! whom I could most have

wished

To live and to be happy, those to perish! Ulysses to sur-
vive! It should not be.

NEOPTOLEMUS Oh! 'tis a subtle foe; but deepest plans
May sometimes fail.

PHILOCTETES Where was Patroclus then, Thy father's
dearest friend?

NEOPTOLEMUS He too was dead. In war, alas- so fate
ordains it ever- The coward 'scapes, the brave and virtuous
fall.

PHILOCTETES It is too true; and now thou talkst of
cowards,

Where is that worthless wretch, of readiest tongue, Subtle and voluble?

NEOPTOLEMUS Ulysses?

PHILOCTETES No;   Thersites, ever talking, never
heard.

NEOPTOLEMUS I have not seen him, but I hear he
lives.

PHILOCTETES I did not doubt it: evil never dies; The
gods take care of that. If aught there be Fraudful and vile,
'tis safe; the good and just Perish unpitied by them. Wherefore is it? When gods do ill, why should we worship them?

NEOPTOLEMUS Since thus it is, since virtue is oppressed,

And vice triumphant, who deserve to live Are doomed to
perish, and the guilty reign. Henceforth, O son of Poeas! far
from Troy And the Atreidae will I live remote. I would not
see the man I cannot love. My barren Scyros shall afford me
refuge, And home- felt joys delight my future days. So, fare
thee well, and may th' indulgent gods Heal thy sad wound,
and grant thee every wish Thy soul can form! Once more,

farewell! I go, The first propitious gale.

PHILOCTETES What! now, my son? So soon?

NEOPTOLEMUS Immediately; the time demands We should be near, and ready to depart.

PHILOCTETES Now, by the memory of thy honoured sire, By thy loved mother, by whate'er remains On earth most dear to thee, oh! hear me now, Thy suppliant! Do not, do not thus forsake me, Alone, oppressed, deserted, as thou seest, In this sad place, I shall, I know it must, be A burthen to thee. But, oh! bear it kindly; For ever doth the noble mind abhor Th' ungenerous deed, and loves humanity; Disgrace attends thee if thou dost forsake me, If not, immortal fame rewards thy goodness. Thou mayst convey me safe to Oeta's shores In one short day; I'll trouble you no longer. Hide me in any part where I may least Molest you. Hear me! By the guardian god Of the poor suppliant, all-protecting Jove, I beg. Behold me at thy feet, infirm, And wretched as I am, I clasp thy knees. Leave me not here then, where there is no mark Of human footstep- take me to thy home! Or to Euboea's port, to Oeta, thence Short is the way to Trachin, or the banks Of Spercheius' gentle stream, to meet my father, If yet he lives; for, oh! I begged him oft By those who hither came, to fetch me hence- Or is he dead, or they neglectful bent Their hasty course to their own native soil. Be thou my better guide! Pity and save The poor and wretched. Think, my son, how frail And full of danger is the state of man- Now prosperous, now adverse. Who feels no ills Should therefore fear them; and when fortune smiles Be doubly cautious, lest destruction come Remorseless on him, and he fall unpitied.

CHORUS (singing) Oh, pity him, my lord, for bitterest woes

And trials most severe he hath recounted; Far be such sad distress from those I love! Oh! if thou hat'st the base Atreidae, now Revenge thee on them, serve their deadliest foe; Bear the poor suppliant to his native soil; So shalt thou bless thy friend, and 'scape the wrath Of the just gods, who still protect the wretched.

NEOPTOLEMUS Your proffered kindness, friends, may cost you dear;

When you shall feel his dreadful malady Oppress you sore, you will repent it.

LEADER OF THE CHORUS Never Shall that reproach be ours.

NEOPTOLEMUS In generous pity Of the afflicted thus to be o'ercome Were most disgraceful to me; he shall go. May the kind gods speed our departure hence, And guide our vessels to the wished-for shore!

PHILOCTETES O happy hour! O kindest, best of men! And you my dearest friends! how shall I thank you? What shall I do to show my grateful heart? Let us be gone! But, oh! permit me first To take a last farewell of my poor hut, Where I so long have lived. Perhaps you'll say I must have had a noble mind to bear it. The very sight to any eyes but mine Were horrible, but sad necessity At length prevailed, and made it pleasing to me.

LEADER One from our ship, my lord, and with him comes A stranger. Stop a moment till we hear Their business with us. (The Spy enters, dressed as a merchant. He is accompanied by one of NEOPTOLEMUS'men.)

SPY Son of great Achilles, Know, chance alone hath brought me hither, driven By adverse winds to where thy vessels lay, As home I sailed from Troy. There did I meet This my companion, who informed me where Thou mightst be found. Hence to pursue my course And not to tell thee what concerns thee near Had been ungenerous, thou perhaps meantime Of Greece and of her counsels naught suspecting, Counsels against thee not by threats alone Or words enforced, but now in execution.

NEOPTOLEMUS Now by my virtue, stranger, for thy news I am much bound to thee, and will repay Thy service.

Tell me what the Greeks have done.

SPY A fleet already sails to fetch thee back, Conducted by old Phoenix, and the sons Of valiant Theseus.

NEOPTOLEMUS Come they then to force me? Or am I to be won by their persuasion?

SPY I know not that; you have what I could learn.

NEOPTOLEMUS And did the' Atreidae send them?

SPY Sent they are, And will be with you soon.

NEOPTOLEMUS But wherefore then Came not Ulysses? Did his courage fail?

SPY He, ere I left the camp, with Diomede On some important embassy sailed forth In search-

NEOPTOLEMUS Of whom?

SPY There was a man- but stay, Who is thy friend here, tell me, but speak softly.

NEOPTOLEMUS (whispering to him) The famous Philoctetes.

SPY Ha! begone then! Ask me no more- away, immediately!

PHILOCTETES What do these dark mysterious whispers mean? Concern they me, my son?

NEOPTOLEMUS I know not what He means to say, but I would have him speak Boldly before us all, whate'er it be.

SPY Do not betray me to the Grecian host, Nor make me speak what I would fain conceal. I am but poor- they have befriended me.

NEOPTOLEMUS In me thou seest an enemy confest To the Atreidae. This is my best friend Because he hates them too; if thou art mine, Hide nothing then.

SPY Consider first.

NEOPTOLEMUS I have.

SPY The blame will be on you.

NEOPTOLEMUS Why, let it be: But speak, I charge thee.

SPY Since I must then, know, In solemn league combined, the bold Ulysses And gallant Diomede have sworn by force Or by persuasion to bring back thy friend: The Grecians heard Laertes' son declare His purpose; far more resolute he seemed Than Diomede, and surer of success.

NEOPTOLEMUS But why the' Atreidae, after so long time, Again should wish to see this wretched exile, Whence this desire? Came it from th' angry gods To punish thus their inhumanity?

SPY I can inform you; for perhaps from Greece Of late you have not heard. There was a prophet, Son of old Priam, Helenus by name, Hlim, in his midnight walks, the wily chief Ulysses, curse of every tongue, espied; Took him. and led him captive. to the Creeks A welcome spoil. Much he foretold to all, And added last that Troy should never fall Till Philoctetes from this isle returned. Ulysses heard, and instant promise gave To fetch him hence; he hoped by gentle means To gain him; those successless, force at last Could but compel him. He would go, he cried, And if he failed his head should pay th' forfeit. I've told thee all, and warn thee to be gone, Thou and thy friend, if thou wouldst wish to save him.

PHILOCTETES And does the traitor think he can persuade me?

As well might he persuade me to return From death to life, as his base father did.

SPY Of that know not: I must to my ship. Farewell, and may the gods protect you both! (The Spy departs.)

PHILOCTETES Lead me- expose me to the Grecian host! And could the insolent Ulysses hope With his soft flatteries e'er to conquer me? No! Sooner would I listen to the voice Of that fell serpent, whose envenomed tongue Hath lamed me thus. But what is there he dare not Or say or do? I know he will be here E'en now, depend on't. Therefore, let's away! Quick let the sea divide us from Ulysses. Let us be gone; for well-timed expedition, The task performed, brings safety and repose.

NEOPTOLEMUS Soon as the wind permits us we embark, But now 'tis adverse.

PHILOCTETES Every wind is fair When we are flying from misfortune.

NEOPTOLEMUS True; And 'tis against them too.

PHILOCTETES Alas! no storms Can drive back fraud and rapine from their prey.

NEOPTOLEMUS I'm ready. Take what may be necessary, And follow me.

PHILOCTETES I want not much.

NEOPTOLEMUS Perhaps My ship will furnish you.

PHILOCTETES There is a plant Which to my wound gives some relief; I must Have that.

NEOPTOLEMUS Is there aught else?

PHILOCTETES Alas! my bow I had forgot. I must not lose that treasure. (PHILOCTETES steps into the cave, and brings out his bow and arrows.)

NEOPTOLEMUS Are these the famous arrows then?

PHILOCTETES They are.

NEOPTOLEMUS And may I be permitted to behold, To touch, to pay my adoration to them?

PHILOCTETES In these, my son, in everything that's

mine

Thou hast a right,

NEOPTOLEMUS But if it be a crime, I would not; otherwise-

PHILOCTETES Oh! thou art full Of piety; in thee it is no crime; In thee, my friend, by whom alone I look Once more with pleasure on the radiant sun- By whom I live- who giv'st me to return To my dear father, to my friends, my country: Sunk as I was beneath my foes, once more I rise to triumph o'er them by thy aid: Behold them, touch them, but return them to me, And boast that virtue which on thee alone Bestowed such honour. Virtue made them mine. I can deny thee nothing: he, whose heart Is grateful can alone deserve the name Of friend, to every treasure far superior.

NEOPTOLEMUS Go in.

PHILOCTETES Come with me; for my painful wound Requires thy friendly hand to help me onward. (They go into the cave.)

CHORUS (singing, strophe 1)

Since proud Ixion, doomed to feel The tortures of th' eternal wheel, Bound by the hand of angry Jove, Received the due rewards of impious love; Ne'er was distress so deep or woe so great As on the wretched Philoctetes wait; Who ever with the just and good, Guiltless of fraud and rapine, stood, And the fair paths of virtue still pursued; Alone on this inhospitable shore, Where waves for ever beat and tempests roar, How could he e'er or hope or comfort know, Or painful life support beneath such weight of woe?

(antistrophe 1)

Exposed to the inclement skies, Deserted and forlorn he lies, No friend or fellow-mourner there To soothe his sorrows and divide his care, Or seek the healing plant of power to 'suage His aching wound and mitigate its rage; But if perchance, awhile released From torturing pain, he sinks to rest, Awakened soon, and by sharp hunger prest, Compelled to wander forth in search of food, He crawls in anguish to the neighbouring wood; Even as the tottering infant in despair Who mourns an absent mother's kind supporting care.

(strophe 2)

The teeming earth, who mortals still supplies With every good, to him her seed denies; A stranger to the joy that flows From the kind aid which man on man bestows; Nor food, alas! to him was given, Save when his arrows pierced the birds of heaven; Nor e'er did Bacchus' heart-expanding bow! For ten long years relieve his cheerless soul; But glad was he his eager thirst to slake In the unwholesome pool, or ever-stagnant lake.

(antistrophe 2)

But now, behold the joyful captive freed; A fairer fate, and brighter days succeed: For he at last hath found a friend Of noblest race, to save and to defend, To guide him with protecting hand, And safe restore him to his native land; On Spercheius' flowery banks to join the throng Of Malian nymphs, and lead the choral song On Oeta's top, which saw Alcides rise, And from the flaming pile ascend his native skies. (NEOPTOLEMUS and PHILOCTETES enter from the cave. PHILOCTETES is suddenly seized with spasms of pain. He still holds in his hand the bow and arrows.)

NEOPTOLEMUS Come, Philoctetes; why thus silent? Wherefore

This sudden terror on thee?

PHILOCTETES Oh!

NEOPTOLEMUS Whence is it?

PHILOCTETES Nothing, my son; go on!

NEOPTOLEMUS Is it thy wound That pains thee thus?

PHILOCTETES No; I am better now. O gods!

NEOPTOLEMUS Why dost thou call thus on the gods?

PHILOCTETES To smile propitious, and preserve us- Oh!

NEOPTOLEMUS Thou art in misery. Tell me- wilt thou not?

What is it?

PHILOCTETES O my son! I can no longer Conceal it from thee. Oh! I die, I perish; By the great gods let me implore thee, now This moment, if thou hast a sword. oh! strike, Cut off this painful limb, and end my being!

NEOPTOLEMUS What can this mean, that unexpected thus It should torment thee?

PHILOCTETES Know you not, my son?

NEOPTOLEMUS What is the cause?

PHILOCTETES Can you not guess it?

NEOPTOLEMUS No.

PHILOCTETES Nor I.

NEOPTOLEMUS That's stranger still.

PHILOCTETES My son, my son

NEOPTOLEMUS This new attack is terrible indeed!

PHILOCTETES 'Tis inexpressible! Have pity on me!

NEOPTOLEMUS What shall I do?

PHILOCTETES Do not be terrified, And leave me. Its returns are regular, And like the traveller, when its appetite Is satisfied, it will depart. Oh! oh!

NEOPTOLEMUS Thou art oppressed with ills on every side.

Give me thy hand. Come, wilt thou lean upon me?

PHILOCTETES No; but these arrows take; preserve 'em for me.

A little while, till I grow better. Sleep Is coming on me, and my pains will cease. Let me be quiet. If meantime our foes Surprise thee, let nor force nor artifice Deprive thee of the great, the precious trust I have reposed in thee; that were ruin To thee, and to thy friend.

NEOPTOLEMUS Be not afraid- No hands but mine shall touch them; give them to me.

PHILOCTETES Receive them, son; and let it be thy prayer

They bring not woes on thee, as they have done To me and to Alcides. (PHILOCTETES gives him the bow and arrows.)

NEOPTOLEMUS May the gods Forbid it ever! May they guide our course And speed our prosperous sails!

PHILOCTETES Alas! my son, I fear thy vows are vain. Behold my blood Flows from the wound? Oh how it pains me! Now It comes, it hastens! Do not, do not leave me! Oh! that Ulysses felt this racking torture, E'en to his inmost soul! Again it comes! O Agamemnon! Menelaus! why Should not you bear these pangs as I have done? O death! where art thou, death? so often called, Wilt thou not listen? wilt thou never come? Take thou the Lemnian fire, my generous friend, Do me the same kind office which I did For my Alcides. These are thy reward; He gave them to me. Thou alone deservest The great inheritance. What says my friend? What says my dear preserver? Oh! where art thou?

NEOPTOLEMUS I mourn thy hapless fate.

PHILOCTETES Be of good cheer, Quick my disorder comes, and goes as soon; I only beg thee not to leave me here.

NEOPTOLEMUS Depend on 't, I will stay.

PHILOCTETES Wilt thou indeed?

NEOPTOLEMUS Trust me, I will.

PHILOCTETES I need not bind thee to it By oath.

NEOPTOLEMUS Oh, no! 'twere impious to forsake thee.

PHILOCTETES Give me thy hand, and pledge thy faith.

NEOPTOLEMUS I do.

PHILOCTETES (pointing up to heaven) Thither, oh, thither lead!

NEOPTOLEMUS What sayst thou? where?

PHILOCTETES Above-

NEOPTOLEMUS What, lost again? Why lookst thou thus On that bright circle?

PHILOCTETES Let me, let me go!

NEOPTOLEMUS (lays hold of him) Where wouldst thou go?

PHILOCTETES Loose me.

NEOPTOLEMUS I will not.

PHILOCTETES Oh! You'll kill me, if you do not.

NEOPTOLEMUS (lets him go) There, then; now Is thy mind better?

PHILOCTETES Oh! receive me, earth! Receive a dying man. Here must I lie; For, oh! my pain's so great I cannot rise. (PHILOCTETES sinks down on the earth near the entrance of the cave.)

NEOPTOLEMUS Sleep hath o'ertaken him. See, his head is lain

On the cold earth; the balmy sweat thick drops From every limb, and from the broken vein Flows the warm blood;

let us indulge his slumbers.

CHORUS (singing) Sleep, thou patron of mankind, Great physician of the mind, Who dost nor pain nor sorrow know, Sweetest balm of every woe, Mildest sovereign, hear us now; Hear thy wretched suppliant's vow; His eyes in gentle slumbers close, And continue his repose; Hear thy wretched suppliant's vow, Great physician, hear us now. And now, my son, what best may suit thy purpose Consider well, and how we are to act. What more can we expect? The time is come; For better far is opportunity Seized at the lucky hour than all the counsels Which wisdom dictates or which craft inspires.

NEOPTOLEMUS (chanting) He hears us not. But easy as it is

To gain the prize, it would avail us nothing Were he not with us. Phoebus hath reserved For him alone the crown of victory; But thus to boast of what we could not do, And break our word, were most disgraceful to us.

CHORUS (singing) The gods will guide us, fear it not, my son;

But what thou sayst speak soft, for well thou knowst The sick man's sleep is short. He may awake And hear us; therefore let us hide our purpose. If then thou thinkst as he does- thou knowst whom- This is the hour. At such a time, my son, The wisest err. But mark me, the wind's fair, And Philoctetes sleeps, void of all help- Lame, impotent, unable to resist, He is as one among the dead. E'en now We'll take him with us. 'Twere an easy task. Leave it to me, my son. There is no danger.

NEOPTOLEMUS No more! His eyes are open. See, he moves.

PHILOCTETES (awaking) O fair returning light! beyond my hope;

You too, my kind preservers! O my son! I could not think thou wouldst have stayed so long In kind compassion to thy friend. Alas! The Atreidae never would have acted thus. But noble is thy nature, and thy birth, And therefore little did my wretchedness, Nor from my wounds the noisome stench deter Thy generous heart. I have a little respite; Help me, my son I I'll try to rise; this weakness Will leave me soon, and then we'll go together.

NEOPTOLEMUS I little thought to find thee thus restored.

Trust me, I joy to see thee free from pain, And hear thee speak; the marks of death were on thee, Raise thyself up; thy friends here, if thou wilt, Shall carry thee, 'twill be no burthen to them If we request it.

PHILOCTETES No; thy hand alone; I will not trouble them; 'twill be enough If they can bear with me and my distemper When we embark.

NEOPTOLEMUS Well, be it so; but rise.

PHILOCTETES (rising) Oh I never fear; I'll rise as well as ever.

NEOPTOLEMUS (half to himself) How shall I act?

PHILOCTETES What says my son?

NEOPTOLEMUS Alas! I know not what to say; my doubtful mind-

PHILOCTETES Talked you of doubts? You did not surely.

NEOPTOLEMUS Aye, That's my misfortune.

PHILOCTETES Is then my distress The cause at last you will not take me with you?

NEOPTOLEMUS All is distress and misery when we act Against our nature and consent to ill.

PHILOCTETES But sure to help a good man in misfortunes Is not against thy nature.

NEOPTOLEMUS Men will call me A villain; that distracts me.

PHILOCTETES Not for this; For what thou meanst to do thou mayst deserve it

NEOPTOLEMUS What shall I do? Direct me, Jove! To hide What I should speak, and tell a base untruth Were double guilt.

PHILOCTETES He purposes at last, I fear it much, to leave me.

NEOPTOLEMUS Leave thee! No! But how to make thee go with pleasure hence, There I'm distressed.

PHILOCTETES I understand thee not; What means my son?

NEOPTOLEMUS I can no longer hide The dreadful secret from thee; thou art going To Troy, e'en to the Greeks, to the Atreidae.

PHILOCTETES Alas! what sayest thou?

NEOPTOLEMUS Do not weep, but hear me.

PHILOCTETES What must I hear? what wilt thou do with me?

NEOPTOLEMUS First set thee free; then carry thee, my friend,

To conquer Troy.

PHILOCTETES Is this indeed thy purpose?

NEOPTOLEMUS This am I bound to do.

PHILOCTETES Then am I lost, Undone, betrayed. Canst thou, my friend, do this? Give me my arms again.

NEOPTOLEMUS It cannot be. I must obey the powers who sent me hither; justice enjoins- the common cause demands it,

PHILOCTETES Thou worst of men, thou vile artificer Of fraud most infamous, what hast thou done? How have I been deceived? Dost thou not blush To look upon me, to behold me thus Beneath thy feet imploring? Base betrayer! To rob me of my bow, the means of life, The only means- give 'em, restore 'em to me! Do not take all Alas Alas! he hears me not, Nor deigns to speak, but casts an angry look That says I never shall be free again. O mountains, rivers, rocks, and savage herds! To you I speak- to you alone I now Must breathe my sorrows; you are wont to hear My sad complaints, and I will tell you all That I have suffered from Achilles' son, Who, bound by solemn oath to bear me hence To my dear native soil, now sails for Troy. The perjured wretch first gave his plighted hand, Then stole the sacred arrows of my friend, The son of Jove, the great Alcides; those He means to show the Greeks, to snatch me hence And boast his prize, as if poor Philoctetes, This empty shade, were worthy of his arm. Had I been what I was, he ne'er had thus Subdued me, and e'en now to fraud alone He owes the conquest. I have been betrayed! Give me my arms again, and be thyself Once more. Oh, speak! Thou wilt not? Then I'm lost. O my poor hut! again I come to thee Naked and destitute of food; once more Receive me, here to die; for now, no longer Shall my swift arrow reach the flying prey, Or on the mountains pierce the wandering herd: I shall myself afford a banquet now To those I used to feed on- they the hunters, And I their easy prey; so shall the blood Which I so oft have shed be paid by mine; And all this too from him whom once I deemed Stranger to fraud nor capable of ill; And yet I will not curse thee till I know Whether thou still retainst thy horrid purpose, Or dost repent thee of it; if thou dost not, Destruction wait thee!

LEADER OF THE CHORUS We attend your pleasure, My royal lord, we must be gone; determine To leave, or take him with us.

NEOPTOLEMUS His distress   Doth move me much. Trust me, I long have felt Compassion for him.

PHILOCTETES Oh then by the gods Pity me now, my

son, nor let mankind Reproach thee for a fraud so base.

NEOPTOLEMUS Alas! What shall I do? Would I were still at Scyros! For I am most unhappy.

PHILOCTETES O my son! Thou art not base by nature, but misguided By those who are, to deeds unworthy of thee. Turn then thy fraud on them who best deserve it; Restore my arms, and leave me.

NEOPTOLEMUS Speak, my friends, What's to be done? (ULYSSES enters suddenly.)

ULYSSES Ah! dost thou hesitate? Traitor, be gone! Give me the arms.

PHILOCTETES Ah me! Ulysses here?

ULYSSES Aye! 'tis Ulysses' self That stands before thee.

PHILOCTETES Then I'm lost, betrayed! This was the cruel spoiler.

ULYSSES Doubt it not. 'Twas I; I do confess it.

PHILOCTETES (to NEOPTOLEMUS) O my son! Give me them back.

ULYSSES It must not be; with them Thyself must go, or we shall drag thee hence.

PHILOCTETES And will they force me? O thou daring villain!

ULYSSES They will, unless thou dost consent to go.

PHILOCTETES Wilt thou, O Lemnos! wilt thou, mighty Vulcan!

With thy all-conquering fire, permit me thus To be torn from thee?

ULYSSES Know, great Jove himself Doth here preside. He hath decreed thy fate; I but perform his will.

PHILOCTETES Detested wretch, Mak'st thou the gods a cover for thy crime? Do they teach falsehood?

ULYSSES No, they taught me truth, And therefore, hence- that way thy journey lies. (Pointing to the sea)

PHILOCTETES It doth not.

ULYSSES But I say it must be so.

PHILOCTETES And Philoctetes then was born a slave! I did not know it,

ULYSSES No; I mean to place thee E'en with the noblest, e'en with those by whom Proud Troy must perish.

PHILOCTETES Never will I go, Befall what may, whilst this deep cave is open To bury all my sorrows.

ULYSSES What wouldst do?

PHILOCTETES Here throw me down, dash out my desperate brains

Against this rock, and sprinkle it with my blood.

ULYSSES (to the CHORUS) Seize, and prevent him! (They seize him.)

PHILOCTETES Manacled! O hands! How helpless are you now! those arms, which once Protected, thus torn from you!   (To ULYSSES) Thou abandoned,

Thou shameless wretch! from whom nor truth nor justice, Naught that becomes the generous mind, can flow, How hast thou used me! how betrayed! Suborned This stranger, this poor youth, who, worthier far To be my friend than thine, was only here Thy instrument; he knew not what he did, And now, thou seest, repents him of the crime Which brought such guilt on him, such woes on me. But thy foul soul, which from its dark recess Trembling looks forth, beheld him void of art, Unwilling as he was, instructed him, And made him soon a master in deceit. I am thy prisoner now; e'en now thou meanst To drag me hence, from this unhappy shore, Where first thy malice left me, a poor exile, Deserted, friendless, and though living, dead To all mankind. Perish the vile betrayer! Oh! I have cursed thee often, but the gods Will never bear the prayers of Philoctetes. Life and its joys are thine, whilst I, unhappy, Am but the scorn of thee, and the Atreidae, Thy haughty masters. Fraud and force compelled thee, Or thou hadst never sailed with them to Troy. I lent my willing aid; with seven brave ships I ploughed the main to serve them. In return They cast me forth, disgraced me, left me here. Thou sayst they did it; they impute the crime To thee. And what will you do with me now? And whither must I go? What end, what purpose Could urge thee to it? I am nothing, lost And dead already. Wherefore- tell me, wherefore?- Am I not still the same detested burthen, Loathsome and lame? Again must Philoctetes Disturb your holy rites? If I am with you How can you make libations? That was once Your vile pretence for inhumanity. Oh! may you perish for the deed! The gods Will grant it sure, if justice be their care And that it is I know. You had not left Your native soil to seek a wretch like me Had not some impulse from the powers above, Spite of yourselves, ordained it. O my country! And you, O gods! who look upon this deed, Punish, in pity to me, punish all The guilty band! Could I behold them perish, My wounds were nothing; that would heal them all.

LEADER (to ULYSSES) Observe, my lord, what bitterness of soul

His words express; he bends not to misfortune, But seems to brave it.

ULYSSES I could answer him, Were this a time for words; but now, no more Than this- I act as best befits our purpose. Where virtue, truth, and justice are required Ulysses yields to none; I was not born To be o'ercome, and yet submit to thee. Let him remain. Thy arrows shall suffice; We want thee not! Teucer can draw thy bow As well as thou; myself with equal strength Can aim the deadly shaft, with equal skill. What could thy presence do? Let Lemnos keep thee. Farewell! perhaps the honours once designed For thee may be reserved to grace Ulysses.

PHILOCTETES Alas! shall Greece then see my deadliest foe

Adorned with arms which I alone should bear?

ULYSSES No more! I must be gone.

PHILOCTETES (to NEOPTOLEMUS) Son of Achilles, Thou wilt not leave me too? I must not lose Thy converse, thy assistance.

ULYSSES (to NEOPTOLEMUS) Look not on him; Away, I charge thee! 'Twould be fatal to us.

PHILOCTETES (to the CHORUS) Will you forsake me, friends? Dwells no compassion Within your breasts for me?

LEADER (pointing to NEOPTOLEMUS) He is our master; We speak and act but as his will directs.

NEOPTOLEMUS I know be will upbraid me for this weakness,

But 'tis my nature, and I must consent, Since Philoctetes asks it. Stay you with him, Till to the gods our pious prayers we offer, And all things are prepared for our departure; Perhaps, meantime, to better thoughts his mind May turn relenting. We must go. Remember, When we shall call you, follow instantly. (NEOPTOLEMUS, still with the bow in his hands, goes out with ULYSSES. The lines in the following scene between PHILOCTETES and the CHORUS are chanted responsively.)

PHILOCTETES O my poor hut! and is it then decreed Again I come to thee to part no more, To end my wretched days in this sad cave, The scene of all my woes? For whither now Can I betake me? Who will feed, support, Or cherish Philoctetes? Not a hope Remains for me. Oh! that th' impetuous storms Would bear me with them to some distant clime! For I must perish here.

CHORUS Unhappy man! Thou hast provoked thy fate; thyself alone Art to thyself a foe, to scorn the good, Which wisdom bids thee take, and choose misfortune.

PHILOCTETES Wretch that I am, to perish here alone! Oh! I shall see the face of man no more, Nor shall my arrows pierce their winged prey, And bring me sustenance! Such vile delusions Used to betray me! Oh! that pains like those I feel might reach the author of my woes!

CHORUS The gods decreed it; we are not to blame. Heap not thy curses therefore on the guiltless, But take our friendship.

PHILOCTETES (pointing to the sea-shore) I behold him there;

E'en now I see him laughing me to scorn On yonder shore, and in his hands the darts He waves triumphant, which no arms but these Had ever borne. O my dear glorious treasure! Hadst thou a mind to feel th' indignity, How wouldst thou grieve to change thy noble master, The friend of great Alcides, for a wretch So vile, so base, so impious as Ulysses!

CHORUS justice will ever rule the good man's tongue, Nor from his lips reproach and bitterness Invidious flow. Ulysses, by the voice Of Greece appointed, only sought a friend To join the common cause, and serve his country.

PHILOCTETES Hear me, ye winged inhabitants of air, And you, who on these mountains love to feed, My savage prey, whom once I could pursue; Fearful no more of Philoctetes, fly This hollow rock- I cannot hurt you now; You need not dread to enter here. Alas! You now may come, and in your turn regale On these poor limbs, when I shall be no more. Where can I hope for food? or who can breathe This vital air, when life-preserving earth No longer will assist him?

CHORUS By the gods! Let me entreat thee, if thou dost regard Our master, and thy friend, come to him now, Whilst thou mayst 'scape this sad calamity; Who but thyself would choose to be unhappy That could prevent it?

PHILOCTETES Oh! you have brought back Once more

the sad remembrance of my griefs; Why, why, my friends, would you afflict me thus?

CHORUS Afflict thee- how?

PHILOCTETES Think you I'll e'er return To hateful Troy?

CHORUS We would advise thee to it.

PHILOCTETES I'll hear no more. Go, leave me!

CHORUS That we shall Most gladly. To the ships, my friends; away!(Going) Obey your orders.

PHILOCTETES (stops them) By protecting Jove, Who hears the suppliant's prayer, do not forsake me!

CHORUS (returning) Be calm then.

PHILOCTETES O my friends! will you then stay? Do, by the gods I beg you.

CHORUS Why that groan?

PHILOCTETES Alas! I die. My wound, my wound! Here-after What can I do? You will not leave me! Hear-

CHORUS What canst thou say we do not know already?

PHILOCTETES O'erwhelmed by such a storm of griefs as I am,

You should not thus resent a madman's frenzy.

CHORUS Comply then and be happy.

PHILOCTETES Never, never! Be sure of that. Tho' thun-der-bearing Jove Should with his lightnings blast me, would I go? No! Let Troy perish, perish all the host Who sent me here to die; but, O my friends! Grant me this last request.

CHORUS What is it? Speak.

PHILOCTETES A sword, a dart, some instrument of death.

CHORUS What wouldst thou do?

PHILOCTETES I'd hack off every limb. Death, my soul longs for death.

CHORUS But wherefore is it?

PHILOCTETES I'll seek my father.

CHORUS Whither?

PHILOCTETES In the tomb; There he must be. O Scyros! O my country! How could I bear to see thee as I am- I who had left thy sacred shores to aid The hateful sons of Greece? O misery! (He goes into the cave.)

LEADER OF THE CHORUS (speaking) Ere now we should have taken thee to our ships, But that advancing this way I behold Ulysses, and with him Achilles' son. (NEOPTOLEMUS enters still carrying the bow; he is followed closely by ULYSSES.)

ULYSSES Why this return? Wherefore this haste?

NEOPTOLEMUS I come To purge me of my crimes.

ULYSSES Indeed! What crimes?

NEOPTOLEMUS My blind obedience to the Grecian host And to thy counsels.

ULYSSES Hast thou practised aught Base or unworthy of thee?

NEOPTOLEMUS Yes; by art And vile deceit betrayed th' unhappy.

ULYSSES Whom? Alas! what mean you?

NEOPTOLEMUS Nothing. But the son Of Poeas-

ULYSSES Ha! what wouldst thou do? My heart Misgives me.

NEOPTOLEMUS I have ta'en his arms, and now-

ULYSSES Thou wouldst restore them! Speak! Is that thy purpose?

Almighty Jove!

NEOPTOLEMUS Unjustly should I keep Another's right?

ULYSSES Now, by the gods, thou meanest To mock me! Dost thou not?

NEOPTOLEMUS If to speak truth Be mockery.

ULYSSES And does Achilles' son Say this to me?

NEOPTOLEMUS Why force me to repeat My words so often to thee?

ULYSSES Once to hear them Is once indeed too much.

NEOPTOLEMUS Doubt then no more, For I have told thee all.

ULYSSES There are, remember, There are who may prevent thee.

NEOPTOLEMUS Who shall dare To thwart my purpose?

ULYSSES All the Grecian host, And with them, I.

NEOPTOLEMUS Wise as thou art, Ulysses, Thou talkst most idly.

ULYSSES Wisdom is not thine Either in word or deed.

NEOPTOLEMUS Know, to be just Is better far than to be wise.

ULYSSES But where, Where is the justice, thus unauthorized, To give a treasure back thou ow'st to me, And to my counsels?

NEOPTOLEMUS I have done a wrong, And I will try to make atonement for it.

ULYSSES Dost thou not fear the power of Greece?

NEOPTOLEMUS I fear Nor Greece nor thee, when I am doing right.

ULYSSES 'Tis not with Troy then we contend. but thee-

NEOPTOLEMUS I know not that.

ULYSSES Seest thou this hand? behold, It grasps my sword.

NEOPTOLEMUS Mine is alike prepared, Nor seeks delay.

ULYSSES But I will let thee go; Greece shall know all thy guilt, and shall revenge it. (ULYSSES departs.)

NEOPTOLEMUS 'Twas well determined; always be as wise As now thou art, and thou mayst live in safety. (He approaches the cave and calls.) Ho! son of Poeas! Philoctetes, leave Thy rocky habitation, and come forth.

PHILOCTETES (from the cave) What noise was that? Who calls on Philoctetes? (He comes out.) Alas! what would you, strangers? Are you come

To heap fresh miseries on me?

NEOPTOLEMUS Be of comfort, And bear the tidings which I bring.

PHILOCTETES I dare not; Thy flattering tongue hath betrayed me.

NEOPTOLEMUS And is there then no room for penitence?

PHILOCTETES Such were thy words, when, seemingly sincere,

Yet meaning ill, thou stolst my arms away.

NEOPTOLEMUS But now it is not so. I only came To know if thou art resolute to stay, Or sail with us.

PHILOCTETES No more of that; 'tis vain And useless all.

NEOPTOLEMUS Art thou then fixed?

PHILOCTETES I am; It is impossible to say how firm-ly.

NEOPTOLEMUS I thought I could have moved thee, but I've done.

PHILOCTETES 'Tis well thou hast; thy labour had been vain;

For never could my soul esteem the man Who robbed me of my dearest, best possession, And now would have me listen to his counsels- Unworthy offspring of the best of men! Perish th' Atreidae! perish first Ulysses! Perish thyself!

NEOPTOLEMUS Withhold thy imprecations, And take thy arrows back.

PHILOCTETES A second time Wouldst thou deceive me?

NEOPTOLEMUS By th' almighty power Of sacred Jove I swear.

PHILOCTETES O joyful sound! If thou sayst truly.

NEOPTOLEMUS Let my actions speak. Stretch forth thy hand, and take thy arms again. (As NEOPTOLEMUS gives the bow and arrows to PHILOCTETES, ULYSSES sud-denly enters.)

ULYSSES Witness ye gods! Here, in the name of Greece And the Atreidae, I forbid it.

PHILOCTETES Ha! What voice is that? Ulysses'?

ULYSSES Aye, 'tis I- I who perforce will carry thee to Troy Spite of Achilles' son.

PHILOCTETES (He aims an arrow directly at ULYSS-ES.) Not if I aim

This shaft aright.

NEOPTOLEMUS (laying hold of him) Now, by the gods, I beg thee

Stop thy rash hand!

PHILOCTETES Let go my arm.

NEOPTOLEMUS I will not.

PHILOCTETES Shall I not slay my enemy?

NEOPTOLEMUS Oh, no! 'Twould cast dishonour on us both. (ULYSSES hastily departs.)

PHILOCTETES Thou knowst, These Grecian chiefs are loud pretending boasters, Brave but in tongue, and cowards in the field.

NEOPTOLEMUS I know it; but remember, I restored Thy arrows to thee, and thou hast no cause For rage or for complaint against thy friend.

PHILOCTETES I own thy goodness. Thou hast shown thyself

Worthy thy birth; no son of Sisyphus, But of Achilles, who on earth preserved A fame unspotted, and amongst the dead Still shines superior, an illustrious shade.

NEOPTOLEMUS Joyful I thank thee for a father's praise, And for my own; but listen to my words, And mark me well. Misfortunes, which the gods Inflict on mortals, they perforce must bear: But when, oppressed by voluntary woes, They make themselves unhappy, they deserve not Our pity or our pardon. Such art thou. Thy savage soul, impatient of advice, Rejects the wholesome counsel of thy friend, And treats him like a foe; but I will speak, Jove be my witness! Therefore hear my words, And grave them in thy heart. The dire disease Thou long hast suffered is from angry heaven, Which thus afflicts thee for thy rash approach To the fell serpent, which on Chrysa's shore Watched o'er the sacred treasures. Know beside, That whilst the sun in yonder east shall rise.

Or in the west decline, distempered still Thou ever shalt remain, unless to Troy Thy willing mind transport thee. There
the sons Of Aesculapius shall restore thee- there By my assistance shalt thou conquer Troy. I know it well; for that prophetic sage, The Trojan captive Helenus, foretold It should
be so. "Proud Troy (he added then) This very year must fall;
if not, my life Shall answer for the falsehood." Therefore
yield. Thus to be deemed the first of Grecians, thus By Poeas' favourite sons to be restored, And thus marked out the
conqueror of Troy, Is sure distinguished happiness.

PHILOCTETES O life! Detested, why wilt thou still keep
me here? Why not dismiss me to the tomb! Alas! What can
I do? How can I disbelieve My generous friend? I must consent, and yet Can I do this, and look upon the sun? Can I
behold my friends- will they forgive, Will they associate with
me after this? And you, ye heavenly orbs that roll around
me, How will ye bear to see me linked with those Who have
destroyed me, e'en the sons of Atreus, E'en with Ulysses,
source of all my woes? My sufferings past I could forget; but
oh! I dread the woes to come; for well I know When once
the mind's corrupted it brings forth Unnumbered crimes,
and ills to ills succeed. It moves my wonder much that thou,
my friend, Shouldst thus advise me, whom it ill becomes
To think of Troy. I rather had believed Thou wouldst have
sent me far, far off from those Who have defrauded thee of
thy just right, And gave thy arms away. Are these the men
Whom thou wouldst serve? whom thou wouldst thus compel
me

To save and to defend? It must not be. Remember, O my
son! the solemn oath Thou gav'st to bear me to my native
soil. Do this, my friend, remain thyself at Scyros, And leave
these wretches to be wretched still. Thus shalt thou merit
double thanks, from me And from thy father; nor by succour
given To vile betrayers prove thyself as vile.

NEOPTOLEMUS Thou sayst most truly. Yet confide in
heaven,

Trust to thy friend, and leave this hated place.

PHILOCTETES Leave it! For whom? For Troy and the Atreidae?

These wounds forbid it.

NEOPTOLEMUS They shall all be healed, Where I will carry thee.

PHILOCTETES An idle tale Thou tellst me. surely; dost thou not?

NEOPTOLEMUS I speak What best may serve us both.

PHILOCTETES But, speaking thus, Dost thou not fear the' offended gods?

NEOPTOLEMUS Why fear them? Can I offend the gods by doing good?

PHILOCTETES What good? To whom? To me or to the' Atreidae?

NEOPTOLEMUS I am thy friend, and therefore would persuade thee.

PHILOCTETES And therefore give me to my foes.

NEOPTOLEMUS Alas! Let not misfortunes thus transport thy soul To rage and bitterness.

PHILOCTETES Thou wouldst destroy me.

NEOPTOLEMUS Thou knowst me not.

PHILOCTETES I know th' Atreidae well, Who left me here.

NEOPTOLEMUS They did; yet they perhaps, E'en they, O Philoctetes! may preserve thee.

PHILOCTETES I never will to Troy.

NEOPTOLEMUS What's to be done? Since I can ne'er persuade thee, I submit; Live on in misery.

PHILOCTETES Then let me suffer; Suffer I must; but,

oh! perform thy promise; Think on thy plighted faith, and guard me home Instant, my friend, nor ever call back Troy To my remembrance; I have felt enough From Troy already.

NEOPTOLEMUS Let us go; prepare!

PHILOCTETES O glorious sound!

NEOPTOLEMUS Bear thyself up.

PHILOCTETES I will, If possible.

NEOPTOLEMUS But how shall I escape The wrath of Greece?

PHILOCTETES Oh! think not of it.

NEOPTOLEMUS What If they should waste my kingdom?

PHILOCTETES I'll be there.

NEOPTOLEMUS Alas! what canst thou do?

PHILOCTETES And with these arrows Of my Alcides-

NEOPTOLEMUS Ha! What sayst thou?

PHILOCTETES Drive Thy foes before me. Not a Greek shall dare Approach thy borders.

NEOPTOLEMUS If thou wilt do this, Salute the earth, and instant hence. Away! (HERCULES appears from above, and speaks as he moves forward.)

HERCULES Stay, son of Poeas! Lo to thee 'tis given Once more to see and hear thy loved Alcides, Who for thy sake hath left yon heavenly mansions, And comes to tell thee the decrees of Jove; To turn thee from the paths thou meanst to tread, And guide thy footsteps right. Therefore attend. Thou knowst what toils, what labours I endured, Ere I by virtue gained immortal fame; Thou too like me by toils must rise to glory- Thou too must suffer, ere thou canst be happy; Hence with thy friend to Troy, where honour calls, Where health awaits thee- where, by virtue raised To highest rank,

and leader of the war, Paris, its hateful author, shalt thou
slay, Lay waste proud Troy, and send thy trophies home,
Thy valour's due reward, to glad thy sire On Oeta's top. The
gifts which Greece bestows Must thou reserve to grace my
funeral pile, And be a monument to after-ages Of these all-
conquering arms. Son of Achilles (Turning to NEOPTOLE-
MUS, For now to thee I speak,) remember this, Without his
aid thou canst not conquer Troy, Nor Philoctetes without
thee succeed; Go then, and, like two lions in the field Roaming for prey, guard ye each other well; My Aesculapius will
I send e'en now To heal thy wounds-Then go, and conquer
Troy; But when you lay the vanquished city waste. Be careful that you venerate the gods; For far above all other gifts
doth Jove, Th' almighty father, hold true piety: Whether we
live or die, that still survives Beyond the reach of fate, and
is immortal.

PHILOCTETES (chanting) Once more to let me hear
that wished-for voice, To see thee after so long time, was
bliss I could not hope for. Oh! I will obey Thy great commands most willingly.

NEOPTOLEMUS (chanting) And I.

HERCULES (chanting) Delay not then. For lo! a prosperous wind

Swells in thy sail. The time invites. Adieu! (HERCULES
disappears above.)

PHILOCTETES (chanting) I will but pay my salutations
here,

And instantly depart. To thee, my cave, Where I so long
have dwelt, I bid farewell! And you, ye nymphs, who on the
watery plains Deign to reside, farewell! Farewell the noise
Of beating waves, which I so oft have heard From the rough
sea, which by the black winds driven O'erwhelmed me, shiv-
ering. Oft th' Hermaean mount Echoed my plaintive voice,
by wintry storms Afflicted, and returned me groan for groan.
Now, ye fresh fountains, each Lycaean spring, I leave you
now. Alas! I little thought To leave you ever. And thou sea-

girt isle, Lemnos, farewell! Permit me to depart By thee unblamed, and with a prosperous gale To go where fate demands, where kindest friends By counsel urge me, where all-powerful Jove In his unerring wisdom hath decreed.

CHORUS (chanting) Let us be gone, and to the ocean nymphs

Our humble prayers prefer, that they would all Propitious smile, and grant us safe return.

THE END

Made in United States
North Haven, CT
04 February 2022

15613813R00096